WHISPERED ECHOES

Cover photo, patience, creative inspiration, unconditional love, and support by Deborah O'Brien

Published by:
Holy Love Reiki
12505 SW North Dakota St. #1816
Tigard, Oregon 97223
www.holylovereiki.com

This is a memoir. The stories are true, although the chronology might not be perfect. When I felt like doing so, I changed names or used only a first name.

ISBN: 9781796978063

Dedicated with love to the memory of
Jane Kristine Huhtala and Jack Allen Huhtala

WHISPERED ECHOES

Who speaks for those without a say?

Peter Huhtala

CONTENTS

CHAPTER ONE

KID

ROLLS ROYCE

LONG DIVISION

ECOLA

HAPPY NEW YEAR

CINDER

DINOSAUR COUNTRY

ESCAPE

ROLLS ROYCE

"Relax, and you won't get hurt," advised the large man pressed against my backpack. He gripped my shoulder with his left hand; with his right hand, he held a machete to my throat.

A short, thin, neatly dressed man standing close to Bob said, "It's okay. Just do as you're told."

The big guy said to me, "We're going to back up slowly. We're going up a flight of stairs. Carefully."

I went up the stairs backward, grateful for the hand on my shoulder, freaked out about the machete near my neck. At the top of the stairs, we entered a room. Bob and the smaller man followed.

The small guy held a pistol. He said, "There's no need for the knife now, Gerry. This will be a friendly exchange." He wagged the gun at me. "Right?"

We were in a luxurious apartment: high-quality furniture, tastefully framed artwork, an expensive stereo system—a total contrast with the deteriorated exterior of the apartment building.

Bob and I had been exploring the Haight-Ashbury neighborhood of San Francisco. We walked down Fillmore Street, then took a side street. I wasn't sure which way to go. Buildings bumped against the sidewalk. Gerry had opened a door and grabbed me from behind. Immediately, he had control of my life.

The small guy looked us over. "How old are you? These are dangerous streets, especially for young white guys."

I looked at the gun. "Eighteen," I said. "What's going on? Who are you?"

"Call me Ed. Everything will be fine," he said. "Please pardon our poor manners. Gerry, change the station to rock 'n' roll. Our guests don't seem to be the soul types." He held the gun steady, pointed at me. "Take off the packs and sit on that sofa." He pointed with the gun.

We complied.

Gerry went through our packs. He took a small amount of marijuana and my camera, a 1950s vintage Argus C4 that I'd had for six years. It only cost twenty-five dollars, but I was fond of it.

"Don't take the camera," I implored.

"You don't get to make those decisions," said Ed. "Now you're gonna toss your wallets to Gerry. One at a time." He made eye contact with me. "You first."

After Gerry removed the money, he showed the wallets to Ed.

Ed nodded and said, "Please return their wallets to our guests."

"Why do you do this?" I asked.

"What?" said Ed. "For the money, of course. Unfortunately, you don't seem to have much. Show me anything else you have. I'll have to kill you if you hold back."

Bob shrugged. I showed him the wristwatch that used to be Uncle Arvi's.

"We'll take the watch. Go get it, Gerry."

"Do you have jobs?" I asked.

Surprised, Ed said, "Yeah, I work for the post office. Gerry has one of those trust funds."

"Then why...?" I was curious.

"Look at this stuff. I like to live well."

"Isn't it risky?"

"Yeah, I like that, too."

"How do you keep from getting caught?"

"I'm glad you asked," he replied, smiling.

Gerry produced another handgun, which he pointed our direction. Ed placed his pistol on an antique table with a small drawer. He opened the drawer, removed a pill bottle, and shook out four yellow capsules.

"First," Ed explained, "I'll kill you if you tell anyone about this transaction. Second, you are each about to swallow two of these. No one will listen to your blather once they take hold. You won't even be able to find this place again. Isn't that a good system?"

"You don't need to worry about us," Bob interjected. "You didn't get much from us. Nobody will care. We're just a couple of stupid kids from Oregon."

"I agree with that last part, but you're still going to swallow these pills."

☯

"Nembutal," said Bob. He was such the taciturn Finn. He hadn't spoken since we left Ed and Gerry's place. Once the pills showed enough of the desired effects, which included tunnel vision, Ed put his pistol in his pocket, walked us several blocks away from the apartment, and disappeared. Eventually, we found our way back to Haight-Ashbury proper, and Bob spoke. "Yellow-jackets."

"Think so?" I replied, slowly. I had tried Seconal, a downer known as reds, but never its purportedly stronger cousin, Nembutal. The air was sluggish.

"Yel-low."

Good thinking. They were yellow.

I felt fall-down drunk, except I couldn't fall fast in this molasses air.

We entered an alley between two large wooden buildings. Bob knocked on a door. I could feel the echoes of the knocks. A nose stuck through a little door in the big door. I wanted to laugh, but I couldn't remember how. The nose talked with Bob, then the big door opened. We walked through the opening.

The person behind the door offered us a baggie full of pot. Bob held it open for me to sniff. Even in my pharmaceutically inebriated state, I could tell it was lousy weed, nothing we wanted. Besides, we didn't have any money...

Bob returned the baggie to the nose-man, whose lips moved as he pointed at a doorway. One syllable at a time I heard sounds: "It. Gets. Bet. Her. That. Way." I followed Bob through the doorway, then through another. My sense was he figured if the pot got better the further into the house we went, then that's where he wanted to go. I'll just sit in this creatively stained overstuffed chair until he returns. The air was thinning.

There were a few others in the room, but they weren't talking. The walls were pocked with several uneven holes in the lath and plaster. Marty Balin came in the way Bob had left. He sat in the chair next to me.

"Hi Marty," I said. "What's with all these holes in the wall?"

"They say Janis Joplin lived here, and before that Timothy Leary. The rumor is that there are loads of dope hid in the walls. Now and then, somebody gets a vision of where it's stashed, and they tear into a wall like a treasure hunter." His voice was soothing.

Still slow, I resonated, "Thank you."

"Janis. I sure miss her."

We sat, silently, for a while.

"I need to go. Be sure to try the Numero Uno next door."

I stood, clumsy yet polite. Marty steadied me, and we shook hands.

As Marty Balin had alerted me, there was Number One, smokable synthetic THC, in the next room. When it was offered to me, I inhaled and settled into a soft cushion.

☯

"Buddy, I'm sorry. Can you hear me? You need to pay attention," someone said directly into my ear. I could feel the warm modulating breath.

"I hear you." The yellow-jackets had begun to wear off.

"Your friend, the guy you came here with, is dead."

"Bob?"

"I don't know his name, but he's dead."

"Where?"

"I'll take you."

I followed him through a beaded curtain, then through a doorway. On a bed, in a small room, was what appeared to be a body with a sheet over the head. I pulled back the sheet to unveil the face. It was Bob.

Jumping on the bed, I yelled at Bob. I ordered him to wake up. He did.

In the daylight, I awoke. Bob handed me a glass of water. We were upstairs in the house in Haight-Ashbury. I remembered excitement among the people that witnessed Bob's return to life. They practically carried us up a staircase to a room of our own, with mattresses on the floor.

"Let's meditate before we go," Bob suggested.

We sat in zazen for about twenty minutes. Then we began to tidy up our packs...

"What's that!"

"Oh, this?" Bob held up a supersized bag of pot and tossed it my way. It smelled delightful—sweet and invigorating. "It's from Michoacán. I had some money in my shoe."

"But Ed would have killed you."

"I didn't think he would."

Bob had spent all of the money on the Michoacán. We panhandled as we walked toward downtown. Once we had two dollars in change, we stopped at the first store we came to and bought a quart of orange juice.

We continued panhandling, without much luck.

"Let's try something different," I suggested.

An older woman with nice clothes, jewelry, make-up, and an expensive hairdo walked toward us. I asked her if she would like some orange juice.

"What did you say?" She asked, coming to a full stop.

"I offered you some orange juice. That's pretty silly because you don't know if we've been drinking from the carton. And there might be something else in there besides juice."

"How old are you?"

"Eighteen."

"What's going on?"

We unloaded an abbreviated version of our past twenty-four hours.

"Wait here. Watch that driveway."

We waited a few minutes. A car appeared in the driveway. That can't be her, I thought. The car was a Rolls Royce Silver Shadow, probably a 1969. Then the front-right window descended. It was our friend. She got out and helped us put our packs in the back seat. Bob sat with the packs. I got in front.

In the car, she reached out her hand, "Hello. I am Claire Masefield." I shook her hand and identified Bob and me. She said she'd been at her family's mountain home for a few months. Now she was planning to stay at their house in town, near the Presidio.

"I can give you a lift to the Golden Gate Bridge."

She did as she said, and handed me ten dollars as we got out.

We walked across the bridge. At the viewpoint on the Marin County side, we found a ride to Petaluma—where we got in line. Petaluma's Highway 101-North ramp had nineteen hitchhikers ahead of us. There was nothing to do but wait. It felt like rain would come soon.

After thirty minutes, we were still fifteen back. Dark clouds gathered above us.

In the distance, a woman walked along a gravel road amongst open fields. She walked tall, like an apparition sure of itself. She came directly to Bob and me, and silently pointed out a house beyond where I had first noticed her. She looked about our age. Trusting, we followed her to the house. When we got there, a middleaged woman met us in the front garden.

"I'm Jeanie's mom. Sometimes, she has visions of people in trouble, and brings them home," she said, smiling. She signed to her daughter.

"We're not in trouble," I said. "We're just hitchhiking home."

Lightning flashed, followed immediately by thunder. The sky opened in a torrent as Jeanie's mom moved us onto the covered porch.

"Where's home?"

"Oregon."

She nodded and looked at her daughter so, I realized, Jeanie could read her lips. "Jeanie will show you to your rooms and the shower. Dinner is at seven."

LONG DIVISION

Because I was the youngest, it was easy to trick me. I hadn't lived long enough to know some stuff, and people thought it was fun to fool me into showing that I was gullible. I knew what gullible meant—and it was me.

When I became four, my sister, Jane, was fifteen. She was more than three times as old as me. I knew how to divide because my brother, Jack, who was ten, had taught me to multiply. Multiplication and division were related. I could think it through and figure out that three times four is twelve—and four times four is sixteen. Jane was not four times as old as me; she was three times as old as me, plus extra. I had no idea what to do with the extra. Jack said he wasn't ready to teach about the extra because he couldn't decide whether I should learn about fractions or decimals first.

Jack thought it was better if he continued to teach me how to read instead of how to properly divide. I wanted to learn both but I was the youngest, so I had to wait. I was happy to read, and I was in a hurry to discover more words and combination of words. But numbers seemed easier, and I felt dumb because I didn't understand the way they worked.

Then it got more urgent than ever to learn the rest of division. I needed a way to express changes in division over time.

About six months after I became four, Jane became sixteen. Now she was four times as old as me, when moments prior she had been three times as old as me. Even with my limited knowledge, I could see how important it was to divide using extra. It was weird not knowing. If Jack couldn't help me, maybe Jane would.

"So I figured out when I became four that you were three times as old as me, plus extra," I explained to Jane. "Then when you became sixteen that made you four times as old as me—all of a sudden. When you become twenty-two, I'll be eleven, which will make you two times as old as me, which is less now. Why does more become less and how do I write it down?"

Jane laughed and laughed.

"Am I being gullible?"

Jane laughed some more. She held her tummy like it hurt.

"What do I need to do?"

"You need to consider that you get older."

"You mean like four-and-a-half."

"Yes, that's a way of saying it with a fraction. You're getting older every minute, every second, every nano-second—"

"Nano-second?"

"Yes, and on and on until infinity becomes so small that there is no way to describe it."

I knew about infinity from talking with Jack about the universe. I thought it meant further and bigger than we can imagine. I liked to talk about infinity because it felt like I was giving my imagination exercise, like the way I can lift heavier things as I grow older and bigger.

"Infinity can be smaller than we can imagine?"

"Yes. It's called infinitesimal."

I wrote that down. Then I told Jane about Jack needing to decide whether to teach me division using fractions or using decimals.

"Tell him to teach you long division."

ECOLA

When we were at a picnic in a park called Ecola, Jane took me to a beach by a big dark-colored cliff.

All of a sudden she yelled, "I am the real Jane."

Instantly, someone on the cliff said, "...real Jane."

Startled, I said, "Who is that?"

Again, Jane yelled, "I am the real Jane."

This time the ocean was a little quieter as a voice came from the cliff, "...real Jane...real Jane...real Jane."

"Where are they?" This was spooky.

"Try it," said Jane. "Yell 'I am Peter.'"

I tried it. Nothing happened.

"Louder. As loud as you can."

I yelled.

This time the cliff replied, "Peter...Peter...Peter." The voice grew softer until it was smothered by the sound that the waves made.

"Is that Jack?" They must think I'm gullible.

"Yell 'Jack is stupid,'" Jane suggested.

"Okay, I will." Jack would be unlikely to agree. I yelled as loud as I could, "Jack is stupid."

The cliff replied, "Jack is stupid...is stupid...stupid...stupid."

I stomped my foot in the sand, but the sand moved out of the way. Nonetheless, I demanded, "What's going on?"

The cliff said, "...on...on...on."

Seriously, I was ready to cry or get mad or something.

Jane laughed and said, "It's an echo."

I said, "I thought this park was Ecola."

Jane laughed loud, and the cliff laughed with her.

Just then, Jack came up from behind us. He faced the cliff and hollered, "Ecola, Ecola, Ecola, Ecola..."

The cliff repeated, "Ecola...Ecola...Ecola..."

Jane started hollering the word, too.

Then they got me to holler.

All three of us yelled the word in our voices, and the cliff said "Ecola" over and over again until we couldn't stand it.

Jack said softly, "Now that's an Ecola."

Over the next few months, I was obsessed with the phenomena, whether it be an echo or an Ecola. Jack took me to a rock quarry with an echo, up by where Dad went to high school. Jack showed me how to find different spots in the quarry where the echoes were longer and clearer. He took me to the Astoria Column where we experimented with echoes up and down the inside of the cylinder.

One day, the whole family took a long trip in the big Chevy. Dad drove. Our mother was in front. Jane and Jack were in back with me. I liked to stand up and look at whatever there was to see.

Jack said we were in the gorge of the Columbia River. I said that gorge sounds like the way Jane eats. Jane walloped me, with knuckles, on my shoulder. Jack put his finger to his lips so I'd know not to yell or cry. I knew he meant that we shouldn't make our mother change.

I sat down between Jane and Jack. I felt sad. Jane and Jack looked sad. Jane kissed my shoulder.

I saw a big waterfall with cliffs the color of the cliffs by the beach.

"Dad," I said, excited. "Can we stop and see if there's an Ecola?"

"We're not stopping until we get to The Dalles," growled our mother.

Pretty soon we came to a tunnel.

"Roll the windows down back there," said Dad.

We did. Dad started honking the horn. The tunnel answered with horn sounds. I squealed, but Jane and Jack got me to calm down.

Our mother said, "Stop that, George!"

We were already out of the tunnel. I could see Dad grinning in the rearview mirror. He could see me back.

I slept. I don't know for how long. Outside the car, the hills looked brown, light brown. The wide, deep, relatively calm Columbia River now had rapids and pools, little waterfalls and eddies.

Dad and Jack were the only ones in the car, besides me.

"Listen carefully," said Jack.

I heard a distant low-pitched sound. It was getting louder. I saw people standing along the shoreline and on rocky outcroppings in the river. They had dip-nets with long poles.

I looked closely. Some platforms and ladders looked like they were held together with rope.

Every moment, one or another fisherman caught a salmon with his net. They'd toss their catch into large baskets.

The roar was almost overwhelming. We got out of the car to watch. We walked a little ways toward the largest falls. Spray from the wild river coated my arms and face.

These fishermen were the Indians that Jack had told me about. He said the next time we go to The Dalles all of these rapids, waterfalls, and fishing spots will be underwater.

We got back into the car and rolled up the windows. When the last part of the final window closed, the roar of Celilo Falls became more like a howl.

"The roar is so loud," explained Jack, "because, first, the water falls on rocks to make the original sounds, then those sounds echo off the rocks and cliffs, which adds to the original sound until we have a cacophony."

"What will happen to these sounds and echoes," I asked, "when all of this is underwater?"

"An excellent question," said Jack.

HAPPY NEW YEAR

The night after I became five I was frightened by Happy New Year. I heard he planned to drive Old Year away. I took a nap, but I hoped I would wake up to say goodbye to Old Year.

I woke up to gunfire! I thought that Happy New Year was shooting at Old Year. I ran out the front door to save Old Year. More gunfire, and bombs! People waved burning sticks.

I asked a man where Old Year was. He told me he was almost gone. I thought he meant that Old Year was dying. I ran to Dad to see if he could help me save Old Year. I told him what the man said.

"Can he live at our house?" Something had to be done. Quickly.

Dad picked me up and carried me inside. He said that Old Year was glad to leave and Happy New Year didn't want to hurt him.

"But what about the guns and bombs?"

"People welcome the New Year by making noise with firecrackers and seal bombs."

"What are seal bombs?"

"Fishermen light them and throw them in the river to break the seals' eardrums and make them drown."

Which question should come first: What is a seal eardrum? How could a bomb find it? What is drown? Why is this the fishermen's job? Does Grandpa throw seal bombs when he goes fishing? Will my eardrum break because I heard them? What are firecrackers? Did my mother bake them?

I ventured, "Does Grandpa know Old Year?"

CINDER

"Why does Cinder sleep in Jane's room?" It wasn't the first time I'd asked the question.

"Because Jane is the oldest," said my mother, wearily. "Now stop asking that."

It's true. Jane was the eldest of us kids. She was sixteen. Jack was eleven. I was five, and so was Cinder, our black Cocker Spaniel.

I think Cinder would like to sleep in the room that Jack and I shared. Cinder loved me, and I loved her. We hugged each other. We wrestled. When I felt like no one else cared about me one little bit, Cinder always cared.

"Cinder is not your dog, Peter. She belongs to Jane and Jack. Get your pajamas on."

What did she know?

The other issue was the Boogie Man. Our mother mentioned this monster-entity just about every night. She advised us to be afraid, warning that it would come out from under our beds if we were bad.

I think Jack was afraid. He didn't want to turn off the ceiling light from the switch by the door and have to walk to his bed in the dark. He rigged up a series of eye-screws and ran fishing line through them. One end of the line was taped to the switch; the other was by his bed. Maybe he wasn't scared. He was an inventor.

I wasn't sure about the Boogie Man. Jane told me that there was no Boogie Man. She said our mother lied to us for fun. But Jane said that there were worse monsters outside, and we needed to be careful of them, especially in the dark when it's raining.

Every night, I checked under our beds, then got into mine. Jack would pull the line to turn off the light, although sometimes he'd read for a while first. There were times when he would fall asleep with the light on. Then I would get up to turn it off, risking that the Boogie Man would grab my feet. But it never happened.

The only times I sensed the presence of something like the Boogie Man was when our mother came into our room at night. I had to close my eyes and cover my head with the blanket while she talked to Jack. That's when I felt scared of monsters.

Christmas had come not long ago, about the same time as my birthday. I got a miniature farm set, with a barn, fences, cows, and horses. That was okay. I picked it out from the Sears catalog in exchange for keeping a secret for my mother.

Auntie Irma and Uncle Arvi gave me plastic dinosaurs. I loved them. I fed cows to the ones with long teeth. Cinder was skittish about them at first, but, eventually, she would lick them. I loved to hug Cinder.

It rained all the time. It splashed in drips and sheets on the big picture window in the dining room. When I went outside, I got all wet. The new jeans I got at Christmas time were too long. The cuffs soaked up water, and they dragged behind me.

Almost every morning, my mother would take me to Auntie Irma's, and I would run from the car to the porch of the big house they called The Craftsman. My mother drove away. I rang the doorbell. I loved ringing doorbells.

Auntie Irma and Uncle Arvi had a son, my cousin, Jimmy. He was away at college, but when he was home, he was lots of fun. He had a machine that played records he called 78s and 45s. He played a song about seventy-six trombones. I liked The Four Freshmen and Elvis Presley.

The people in that house listened to me. They answered my questions. They seemed interested in me, instead of super-tired of hearing things, like my mother was. At that house, I felt what I felt when I hugged Cinder: Relief.

They had paintings and other wonderful things. They had knickknacks that made my breath do something strange. I didn't know it was called awe.

The Craftsman was across from an elementary school. In the morning, I looked out the leaded glass window at children arriving in the rain. In the afternoon, I watched the children return to the rain.

On one of those rainy afternoons, tragedy arrived.

The students had just dispersed. I was about to walk away from the window, but I saw my mother driving down the hill. She parked pointing down, but with the car on the left-hand side in front of The Craftsman.

She opened the big door of the old coupe and pulled out a bag. She walked toward the porch, leaving the car door open. Cinder jumped out of the car. I was excited to see my good friend.

Auntie Irma had popped out the kitchen door. Maybe she was going to get the bag.

I put on my coat and opened the front door.

Auntie Irma screamed. I'd never heard such a scream.

Another car was stopped in the middle of the road alongside the car that my mother had parked. A man opened the driver's door of the car.

I ran out to see what was happening. Then I saw Cinder. She laid on the pavement. She wasn't moving.

I entered a bubble of space-time. The situation was depicted fully, in slow-motion if I preferred. The car the man drove hit Cinder hard enough that she flew through the air as the brakes were applied. She landed on the road. Then the car accelerated and hit her again.

The man stumbled as he got out of his car.

The adults noticed me.

"Get him out of here," yelled my mother.

Auntie Irma apparently thought that was a good idea. She took me away in her car.

"I'm sorry," she said.

"Why are you sorry?"

"I mean I'm sad for you. I'm sad that you lost your dog."

"I know where Cinder is."

"Yes, Pekka Poika, but now she is dead." She called me by my Finnish name. Usually, this signaled trouble if my mother used it. But my Auntie sounded sweet... Dead?

"What do you mean? She's by your house."

"You don't understand, do you? Cinder has gone to Heaven."

"Is that bad?"

"Well, no. But we won't see her again. That's what is sad."

"I want to see Cinder again," I sobbed.

I felt terrible. I had a huge sorrow mixed with super anger.

He will have to die.

"Will the police men come? He killed Cinder, and he'll have to be punished with death. Do police men come, or do we bring him downtown to be hanged? How does this work?"

Irma was driving back to her house. Quickly.

"What about my mother?"

"What?"

"She left the door open. She is guilty, too. It took both of them. Do you think they planned to kill Cinder?"

I saw Dad throw Cinder into the back of his pickup.

"Go. Go!" I could hear my mother yelling.

Dad drove away. Auntie Irma parked. I jumped out.

"Where did Dad take Cinder?" I demanded. I wanted to hug my dog.

It took a while, but my mother finally told me that Dad had gone to bury Cinder in our rose garden.

It felt like the world had punched me in the belly with all it had.

I must have cried for hours. I remember getting dragged to our bedroom and left on the floor. Jack had fallen asleep with the light on. I closed the door. I stopped crying.

My plan refreshed me. I waited. I listened. Jane turned off her little radio. Our mother and Dad made the sounds of going to sleep. I quietly left the room, walked across the kitchen in the dark, then down the basement stairs.

I arrived at the small rose garden in the heavy rain. I could sense where the ground was disturbed. I got on my knees and dug with my hands and arms. The grave was shallow, but the soil was wet and sticky.

I tugged and tugged, and finally pulled Cinder from the ground. I hugged her for as long as it took.

DINOSAUR COUNTRY

Doctor Palmrose lived at the edge of the Big Woods. That's what Jack called the evergreen forest that rolled through Astoria and a bunch of the Pacific Northwest. In my imagination, the forest sprawled to Canada, Alaska, and Chicago.

At age five I wouldn't enter the Big Woods by myself, even if I was somehow granted authority. Jack informed me of actual inhabitants of the forest that included cougar, bear, and mountain beaver. Jane described evil creatures and dark forces.

I associated Doctor Palmrose with the smelly salves and out-of-reach pills that were distributed to my siblings when they had coughs or fevers. Jack attempted to explain these substances as special mixtures of chemicals—similar to laundry detergent, lacquer thinner, and pepper.

I pictured the doctor mixing secret concoctions in that house at the edge of the forest. I saw him wearing a white laboratory coat, similar to that worn by a character in a scary show that Jane encouraged me to watch on our green-tinted television.

Sometimes Dad took me to a doctor's office downtown, but never to Doctor Palmrose. No one explained the reason, but I was okay with the status quo particularly after the sign appeared.

Jack, destined to be a great educator, taught me to read, starting when I became four. I did well with small words and the names of dinosaurs.

My reading abilities awakened concerns about Doctor Palmrose's place. Tall cedar, hemlock, and fir trees bumped against it. There was also a spring that appeared in the woods and flowed near his house. It descended from the property in a miniature cascade with assembled basalt and a little waterfall. Then it disappeared beneath the street.

The sign came to my attention when I waited in the car while my mother went up to the doctor's house to pick up chemicals or something. It said: "Water is Not Safe to Drink" or a close approximation. It was installed in an official manner next to the cascade. I could read. I was concerned. I suspected that something happened to the water as it passed Doctor Palmrose's place. Maybe he put chemicals from his laboratory into it. He might be so powerful and dangerous that no one could stop him from poisoning the water. The best that the people who take care of the town—the street cleaner, the Mayor—could do is to put up the sign.

I planned to discuss this situation with Jack, later that day, but he was busy with homework, which oddly had to do with school rather than home. Jane was on a date. Dad was very sleepy. I was afraid that my mother would tell the doctor that I was on the case so I couldn't tell her. It was good that Jack and Jane were the only ones who knew I could read.

The next day brought another serious matter.

My buddy Jeff lived about a half-block away. We were exactly the same age—five. He came over in the morning. We messed around in a patch of fast-growing Japanese knotweed, a dense imaginary jungle where we could quickly disappear.

"Stay out of that stuff," my mother yelled from the house.

Jeff and I obeyed. What can we do? I had plastic dinosaurs. Whatever we did, we needed to include them.

The town had several urban deciduous forests of alder, maple, and elderberry. Some had various shrubs, salmonberry and huckleberry bushes, and blackberry vines. We called these the Little Woods.

From my side-yard across a gravel section of Pleasant Avenue, we could see a hillside covered in a near-monoculture of young alder, a type of Little Woods. I asked Jeff if he had been there. He hadn't. I hadn't gone there either. It looked like a fun place to explore, especially with two of us.

We didn't have permission to cross the road but cross the road we did, dinosaurs in hand. We climbed the hill.

"Let's pretend this is Dinosaur Country." I'm not sure who said it, but we both agreed. It was different from any other place I'd known. We climbed. We called out the names of dinosaurs that we pretended to see. Stegosaurus. Brontosaurus. Triceratops. We avoided any mention of Tyrannosaurus Rex. Just in case.

We were both high on the hill when it appeared: A great blue heron. Neither Jeff nor I were familiar with this bird. Clearly, to us, it was a pterodactyl.

We looked at each other. I articulated the obvious, "We imaginated too hard."

We had to get out of there if it was even possible. We dashed down the hill. At one point I stumbled and scraped my knee. But there was no time to waste. We had to make it home before... Before what? We could be carried away by the pterodactyl. We might be chewed in the jaws of T-Rex.

Seriously, I wasn't sure if making it home would break the spell. We were on the road, and the pterodactyl was still sailing along.

I got to my house, but I didn't want to go inside. I vacillated between saving my life and the volatile consequences of explaining to my mother what had happened.

Jeff flew on past. "See you tomorrow."

My mother opened the door and looked my way, focussing on my jeans.

"What did you do to your pants? They were almost new. Paha poika." Bad boy.

Yeah, I guess. My knee was throbbing, aching, and bleeding on my jeans. I was back from Dinosaur Country and in trouble.

Two weeks later, I was taking a bath. I marveled at how my scraped up knee had healed. But there was still a little bump that itched. I scratched at it, and it popped. White fluid dripped out. What was it?

Jack had explained blood a couple of times, at least. I didn't fully understand, but I knew it was important. He never told me about this white stuff, but I figured it had an important function as well.

The bump still itched. I pinched it, and something started to come out of my knee. Desperate, I tried to shove it back in. But that hurt. I pulled on it, and it came out, and out further until it was completely removed from my body.

Oh no! I broke my body. This thing was as long as my knee-cap was wide. Straight. White. Solid. It must be important. Have I ruined my life?

Jack thought it was a bone, but admitted that he didn't know a lot about the bones of the knee.

I needed help. I got dressed, combed my hair, and took some deep breaths. I brought the bone thing and went to talk with my mother.

"You need to take me to the doctor downtown. Or to the hospital where I was born."

"Don't be silly. You're making things up."

We went back and forth for what felt like forever. Then I had an idea.

"Help me, or I'll go to the mailman and have him send me to new parents."

Oddly, that worked. She went to the rotary phone and dialed.

After talking, she returned to me and said, "The public nurse won't be there until Monday. This is Saturday."

"Then have the operator call the hospital. I have to save my body."

"Go to your room and wait."

I waited. Maybe she did take me seriously.

She opened my door.

"Get in the car," she said, "and never make me do something like this ever again."

Fine.

“Where are we going?”

“To Doctor Palmrose’s house.”

What a mix of emotions! I was terrified that I’d removed part of my body that was essential for its continued operation. I relied on an unpredictable parent. I was on my way, with that parent, to the abode of a suspected mad scientist. Two weeks ago I had seen a prehistoric flying reptile. I was five.

Doctor Palmrose was not wearing his lab coat. He wore a casual sweatshirt. I could sense his kindness. As I gave him my body part, I almost pulled back at the last moment. Instead, I mustered trust.

As my mother and I waited in the kitchen, she drifted into her world; not Dinosaur Country, someplace else. When the doctor returned, he gestured for me to follow him down the hall. We entered his study, and he pulled the door shut behind us. He sat at his huge desk. I bumped my chest against the other side of the desk.

“I’ve solved part of the mystery,” he said as he slipped my body part from an opaque envelope, “I had to break it—”

“What!” My heart sunk into the hardwood floor. I would never be whole.

“Peter,” he said softly. “It’s wood. A stick.”

“Wood?”

“We need to know how it got your white blood cells on it. Did someone stick you with a splinter of wood?”

“No.” Oh, there are white blood cells.

I told him what had happened. I showed him my knee. He could see the place where the stick came out of my knee. He showed me where it had entered and journeyed under my knee cap for two weeks. He still seemed to think that someone had done this to me. He didn’t believe in dinosaurs.

“Sir Doctor?”

“Yes.”

“Why did they put that sign by the creek, about the water not being safe?”

“I put up the sign. Deer sometimes pee or poo in the water.

People can get sick if they drink the water. I wanted to let everyone know."

He sized me up.

"How did you know what the sign said?"

"I can read."

"Please tell your friends.

☯

Within the year, I had one more encounter with Doctor Palmrose. My mother accidentally slammed my thumb in the car door. Accidentally means she didn't plan to do it, even though she did it with all her might.

We were near the doctor's downtown office. I didn't even know he had an office, but there we were.

Mother sat in the waiting room. I followed Doctor Palmrose down the hall. He asked me to wait in an empty room while he gathered his supplies.

When he returned he had a wad of gauze in one hand; in the other, he held the largest pair of pointed scissors that I'd ever seen.

I dashed between his legs. I ran down the hall, through the waiting room, out the door, and down the sidewalk. When I reached the river, I scrabbled along the rip rap to a place where I could enter the dark spaces beneath the town. I could, but I didn't.

I didn't know what to do. I felt deeply lonely. If only I could find Dad. I'll tell him what happened. He'll believe me. He'll protect me. I have hope. That's what I said to the terrible feeling in my belly. It didn't help.

Then the police showed up.

"Am I glad to see you. My mother and Doctor Palmrose are in a conspiracy to cut off my thumb. I don't know why. Maybe they want to sell it. My mother wants money a lot. I thought Doctor Palmrose was okay, but I guess you're going to have to go to his house and search for a secret laboratory. I'm so glad you're here and on the case. My thumb is fine. You can find Dad and figure out a place to meet so we can be together while you track down my mother and Doctor Palmrose and put them in the jail."

They laughed.

Shortly after that, they tried to turn me over to my mother, who waited in our car. I kicked and screamed and wouldn't stay in the vehicle. Finally, one of the police officers convinced me that my thumb was safe now that they knew about it. He drove me home in a police car. Dad was there. He didn't say I was bad. He said he didn't blame me. And even though it was a good story, and oh how he loved good stories, he promised never to tell it in front of me.

ESCAPE

I ruined my chance to go to kindergarten.

Late in spring, when there hadn't been much rain, I left. I intended to leave forever. Even before I escaped, I felt terrible that I wouldn't see some people anymore. But this is how it had to be. I was suffocating. It was like there was a boulder on my chest. If I couldn't escape, it wouldn't matter if we saw each other.

My mother went to the store, leaving no one at the house but me. I wrapped a jacket, some crackers, my dinosaurs, and not much else in a blanket. I unscrewed the long round stick from a broom and tried to tie my blanket to one end, the way I imagined hobos did. It didn't work.

There wasn't much time. I put the stick in the closet, scooped up my blanket of stuff, and went out the door. I looked straight ahead as I walked to the Big Woods. If I didn't see anyone maybe they wouldn't see me.

Stepping into the Big Woods was like crossing into another dimension. And I did it! A short walk into the dark forest brought me to a small stream. I realized that I hadn't brought anything to drink. It was good to know that the world beyond Pleasant Avenue would have streams with water to drink.

An owl screeched.

It would probably be good, I figured, as fear trickled about in my heart, if I came out of the woods for a short time. I climbed a nearby clay hill that was still in full sunshine.

As I sat on the hill, I decided to make some plans. For one, it might be a good idea to walk on the streets and the trails between the houses. That way, I'd have more light than there is in the Big Woods.

What if I needed something? I could do stuff. I could trap chipmunks, at least I'd seen it done. I could stack firewood. I could keep secrets.

When I thought about the secrets, my thoughts went blank. My feelings stopped. I couldn't move.

It was completely dark when the police men woke me up. They shined big bright flashlights at me. There were three of them. One had been there when I hid by the river. He was mad at me. Another argued that they should take me somewhere else for questioning because when they asked me things at the hill, I couldn't talk.

They delivered me back to the house.

After the police drove away in their clean cars, my mother yelled at me with a terrifying voice, like nothing I had heard. It was taunting, menacing. She shook and flailed, ran at me, shoved me down, and kicked me.

After this, when I spoke, my voice did something strange. Sounds would repeat like they were revving up to say something.

I didn't go to Auntie Irma's house anymore. I wasn't allowed to play with other kids. I had to be with Dad or my mother always.

Jack was quiet during that time. He looked sad around his mouth. Jane was angry. She yelled at Dad and slammed her bedroom door.

This might have been a bad time in my life, but there were good things. I could read. I could read anything: Jack and Jane's books, catalogs, the *Reader's Digest.*

The other good thing was that I got to be with Dad a lot. He had a workshop that used to be the neighborhood store until the store moved across the street. He had big machines that made sawdust. He sawed boards, glued, clamped, and nailed. He made boxes that he called cabinets.

I sat in a small chair, so I was out of the way. I was supposed to be quiet most of the time, which was easy because it was hard to talk over the roar of the machines. Besides, I didn't speak much. I liked it when Dad stopped working so he could smoke a Winston cigarette. He would tell me about what he was building, or tell me a joke. I didn't always understand, but it felt good when he spoke to me as if I was older than five.

We had tuna sandwiches or chicken or smoked salmon or hardtack and butter for lunch. I drank milk or sometimes Coca-Cola. Dad drank Olympia beer.

When he finished work for the day, Dad enjoyed more beer and cigarettes. I swept the sawdust and put it in special boxes.

Sometimes Auntie Irma came to the shop and whispered with Dad. She was nice to me. She brought cookies for us. She didn't expect me to talk but tried to listen if I did.

Grandpa came to the shop, too. I loved Grandpa. He spoke Finnish with Dad. He got Dad to laugh. Could anyone get me to laugh? Jack tried; he used jokes from bubblegum wrappers.

"Why can you never go hungry at the beach?"

"Wh-Wh-Why?"

"Because of the sand which is there!"

"H-h-hah, h-h-hah." I wondered how I would sound if I laughed for real.

I was sad that I had caused everyone to be upset. Kindergarten started without me. It was my fault.

I tried to avoid more mistakes, but I failed several times and made my mother's bad voice come out. The others tried, too. Jack stayed quiet and studious. Jane had a boyfriend, and she'd stay away from the house as much as she could. Dad worked and visited friends when he wasn't working. That's what he did when I was with him. Sometimes I stayed in his truck, where I felt safe.

Dad gave me a dime to sweep the shop, and a nickel to pile wood in the special area next to the fireplace in the living room. I'd negotiate for other jobs.

With my own money, I pondered endless options of assorted candy at the neighborhood store. Bob, the proprietor of Astor Court Grocery, tried to fill my ever-changing order but sometimes, when he saw me coming, he put on a face like Dad made when I couldn't stop asking why about everything.

☯

Finally, it was time for First Grade. My first day of school started out awful because my mother insisted that I wear a ridiculous Buster Brown outfit. But I quickly forgot about clothes as the learning began.

I got special counseling for my stutter, from a nice lady.

My friends from Pleasant Avenue and beyond were there. I made new friends, too. School was a relief. Such a relief!

My life was good. So why did I have this new feeling that Jack called "skeptical?"

CHAPTER TWO

SCHOOL

SHOW AND TELL

Only Jane and I knew that Jack walked in his sleep. Jane showed me how to steer him and make him walk in circles. At first, I thought he was faking, but he mostly had his eyes closed. Jane said we shouldn't tell our parents. I don't know why. I didn't tell anyone, even though I thought it might be an interesting topic for Show and Tell.

Show and Tell is a way for kids to learn what each other like, even what they dream they'll become. A kid might bring pictures taken with a Brownie camera. Another kid might bring a plastic fireman's hat or a toy revolver that looks like the ones the police get to shoot. Kids might talk about places they have been, such as New York City, or Warrenton. One kid brought an ant farm, like the one Jack used to have.

For my first Show and Tell I sang "Frère Jacques" in French, to honor my brother, Jack. Somehow, I could restrain my stutter when I sang that song in French but not if I sang it in English.

Kids seemed to like the song, but Jack said I needed to make an impression. I didn't know what he meant. Jack taught me how to spell antidisestablishmentarianism. It wasn't hard to remember the letters and which went after the other. My stutter was a problem, but Jack had an idea: If I sang the letters, maybe I could fend off the stutter. It worked! When I spelled it for the next Show and Tell, I could tell that our first-grade teacher was quiet after I finished because she couldn't choose which thought to say out loud. That was probably an impression.

Kids liked to talk about their cats and dogs during Show and Tell. When they did, I could feel the love they had for their animals. I still love my dog Cinder, even though she was murdered when I was five. Sometimes I cry, but I try not to let anyone know. When I got home after one of the Show and Tell days I accidentally started crying.

"You're whimpering about that dog again. I can see you," my mother said. She pried my hands away from my face so she could find evidence—water coming from my eyes. Evidence meant she could slap my face to make it red.

She grabbed my arm so I couldn't get away when she slapped my face. She said, "This is why you can never have a pet ever again." She slapped me at the same time as she said "never" and "have" and "a pet" and "ever" and "again." At the end of her sentence, she paused, then slapped me again.

"Wh-when I'm tw-twenty-one I-I'll h-have a d-dog," I glared. "And sh-she'll b-bite you, j-just like your d-dead d-dog M-Milo d-did."

Whenever I mentioned Milo, my mother would cry. I knew it would happen, and at first, it made my chest swell like I was strong. Then my feelings would change, quickly. I felt sad in my belly and mad at myself at the same time. The inside of my head throbbed. I didn't want my mother to cry. If it helped, I would tell a judge that I was guilty of making her cry. I would admit it.

I asked my sister, Jane, about my idea of talking to a judge. She was almost a grownup. She might even know somebody who wanted to be a judge.

At first, she looked as though she was going to laugh. She was probably thinking about a joke she'd heard. In a little bit of time, she got really serious. She held my hands and looked at my eyes.

Jane said, and I remember it exactly: "Mom should never slap you. You don't have to say you're guilty to anyone. It's not your fault."

She made a thinking face.

"Some judges are Evil," she said. "Be careful if you find one."

I nodded and slowly took my hands away. Jane knew a lot about Evil. When I was five, she told me that Evil took-over my mother when she hit me with Dad's belt and buckle, and with Dad's ashtray.

Slaps didn't hurt as much as hard things did.

I wondered whether Evil took-over my words when I made my mother cry by tricking her into thinking about her dog, Milo. I knew it would cause bad feelings in her when I made plans to say it. Did that make me Evil? I kept these wonders to myself. Jane had helped me as much as she could.

☯

I went to Captain Robert Gray School, which could be confusing. People call it Gray School for short. Sometimes people say I am in "grade" school, or they ask which grade school I go to because there are more than one. For a long time, I was confused about Gray and grade. That's how stupid I was; I was so stupid I wouldn't even ask someone to explain this anomaly.

It's a good thing that I decided to become a poet. One day, I walked downtown to the public library to look at books about poetry.

There it was! A homonym had fooled me, and it wasn't even an exact homonym. Homonyms, everybody-but-me knew, are words that sound the same but mean different things. I pronounced Gray and grade the same. With my stutter, they both came out Gr-Grae.

Robert Gray was a ship captain. Someone put his name on a school even though he's dead. A grade is a year in school or a school where you attend the first six grades. And grey is a color!

When I got back from that visit to the library, both Jane and Jack were home. I told them how I had been confused and what I'd learned. I didn't remember them ever laughing together, at the same time. Maybe they did when they watched a TV show. But that day they laughed and laughed.

I started thinking that it felt good that I had done something to get them to laugh together, but they interrupted my thinking. They tickled me and tossed me back and forth until...

I found myself laughing!

I had never laughed at myself. I didn't know it could be done. I laughed with my sister and my brother until we fell to the floor.

KHRUSHCHEV'S LOAFER

Premier Khrushchev of Russia slapped his loafer on a table on Columbus Day in 1960. This made grownups worry. They were afraid that Russians would send airplanes with giant bombs to blow up Astoria and Portland and The Dalles.

Dad didn't seem worried about bombs as much as other grownups, such as Mr. Nixon, who was Vice President but wanted to be President, and Jack Kennedy, who was Catholic and also wanted to be President. The men who wanted to be President argued about stuff on TV.

Dad said he was going to bet on Mr. Nixon. I was seven and three quarters, which made me too young to bet. I didn't know why. If I could bet, I'd have chosen Mr. Kennedy because people called him Jack, like my brother's name. But sometimes they called Mr. Kennedy John, which was confusing.

Mr. Nixon lost, so that made Jack Kennedy the President. Dad said, "I always bet on the wrong one."

President Kennedy and Premier Khrushchev argued a lot. People at school said there would be an atomic war, with atom bombs. Our teacher showed us where Russia was on a map of the world.

I held up my hand to be recognized. I asked why Russia and Siberia and Greenland were larger on the map than they were on the globe we had in our classroom, and who was the Premier of Greenland.

The teacher didn't answer. She had us try to climb under our desks so an atom bomb wouldn't hurt us. I think we had the wrong kind of desks.

It seemed like the higher on the hill kids lived, the more their parents worried about atom bombs. A lot of them built secret hideouts so their families could hide from the cosmic rays that atom bombs bring. Their kids weren't supposed to tell anyone that their parents had built the secret hideouts, but the kids bragged at our neighborhood meetings anyway.

I asked Dad to build a secret hideout. Jack said a good place for it would be the workshop in the basement, behind the garage. Dad told us that people who didn't have a secret hideout could stay in the basement of the Post Office. That sounded like more fun than squeezing our family into a little room. What would happen when there was an argument?

Jack knew more than he told me; I could tell by studying his eyes. Jack was almost fourteen, and he had read practically every book. He said we should avoid cosmic rays. He also said that scientists wanted to make big hideouts on the moon.

I asked him why the globe is different from the map. I suspected that the teacher didn't know.

Jack was happy I asked. He got an orange and used his smelly marking pen to draw some countries, including Russia. He said that the orange's navel was the North Pole. Then he peeled the orange real carefully, so there was only one piece of peel when he was done. He pushed on the peel to make it flat like a map. Then he picked it up and made it look sort of like a globe again. Then he made it flat.

"Look," he said. "See where I drew Russia? Now there are empty spaces in the part closest to where the North Pole was. You see bits of the navel here, here, and here. Get it." He could tell I didn't.

He mumbled something about a person named Mercator. He put the orange peel on a piece of paper and drew some lines. Jack was running out of ideas. He got his atlas from his bookshelf and opened it to a page with a picture of a flat earth with ships falling off the edge into outer space.

"We now know that the earth is not flat," he said. "But what if it's not round either?"

"H-how m-many p-people c-can f-fit in the b-basement of the P-post Office?"

“Not enough.”

“W-who is the Pr-premier of Gr-green L-land?”

“I’ll have to research that. Let’s look in the World Almanac.”

JACK ALLEN

Jack was born on December 23, and I was born on December 30 six years later. Our's were not the best days for birthdays.

Usually, I'd get one present that was big enough for my birthday and Christmas together. Once it was a bike from the *Sears Roebuck* catalog. Dad brought it in on Christmas Eve with a red ribbon on the handlebars, tied like a shoelace. Jack helped me move the bike seat down until I could reach the pedals. I was okay a few days later when no one mentioned that they knew it was my birthday.

☯

Jack was an inventor and the smartest person in Oregon. During the year that he was fifteen, he did many amazing things. For his birthday-and-Christmas present, he got a jigsaw. He also got two magazine subscriptions: *Popular Science* and *Popular Mechanics*.

Cousin Jim passed down a microscope for Jack. Jack invented a project to do with the microscope. We found some small jars with lids, and Jack put pieces of masking tape on the lids of each of the jars. We put them in a sack and went on a long walk. When we came to a puddle, Jack took the lid off a jar, wrote something on the masking tape, put some water from the puddle into the jar, and put the lid back on. Then we walked some more.

Jack repeated this at two creeks in the Big Woods, at Tapiola Park, at Youngs Bay, and other places—even near the end of a sewer pipe.

At home, he selected a jar and used an eyedropper to place water from the jar onto a piece of glass he called a slide, then he dropped a small square of clear plastic atop the water. He slipped the slide onto the microscope and turned on its light. He leaned forward to look in the microscope.

"Here," offered Jack. "Take a look."

I did. It looked blurry.

Jack looked in the microscope again and turned a nob.

"Try it now."

Wow. There were things that looked like little animals swimming and wiggling.

Jack told me it was his scientific belief that we would find different animals in each of the jars, depending on where the water came from. He was so smart it almost felt like my head was exploding.

Jack had lots of ideas about what to make with his jigsaw. He liked some pictures he found in books and magazines—animals, trees, boats, and famous people. The problem was the pictures were too small. I tried to help by drawing larger pictures, but they didn't look the way Jack wanted. Then he found a solution in *Popular Mechanics* magazine: He could build a pantograph.

He did it! Jack built a pantograph. Dad gave him plywood, dowels, and sticks. Jack followed the instructions in *Popular Mechanics*. Within a few days, he was done. He had built a machine he could use to trace a small picture of a chipmunk using a nail attached to moving sticks. On the far side of the plywood, where he had attached a pencil to a stick, a drawing appeared on a piece of butcher paper—a much larger drawing that looked just like the chipmunk picture. It was magic!

The next thing I knew, Jack taped the new, large chipmunk drawing onto a thin piece of plywood. He borrowed an awl from Dad and poked holes through the drawing and into the plywood. When he took the paper away, there was a follow-the-dots picture on the plywood.

I stood back while Jack cut the plywood with his jigsaw.

When he finished, he had a big wooden chipmunk. Later, he found some dark brown paint and used it to color his chipmunk. He put it on a shelf in our bedroom.

Now that he had a pantograph, Jack could not be stopped. He could change the size of anything in any book and cut it out with his jigsaw.

By the time the next Christmas-Birthday-Happy New Year season came around Jack had built a Jesus and the Wise Men scene with three dimensions and hidden colored lights. For the most delicate details, he used cardboard. He used paint that he sprayed from a can.

At first, Jane didn't believe that Jack had built the scene, but I told her it was true. Then she was excited, too. She wanted one just like it.

Everyone who saw the scene was impressed, except our mother. The special teacher I saw for stuttering told me that our mother had never learned how to appreciate things that other people did. That's why she gave herself credit when she looked at my report card. I felt sorry for her, but I didn't show her my rhymes.

I hoped Jack didn't feel bad because our mother couldn't praise his inventions. I wanted to talk to him about this and about my troubles. I couldn't. She might really hurt him if she found out I told any part of the secrets.

Jack's extraordinary year didn't stop there. He got Dad to give him a full-sized piece of thick plywood. He traced and drew Santa Claus and cut him out. He painted Santa's suit and hat, and the big bag of Christmas gifts. For Santa's face, Jack used the same dark brown paint that he used for his chipmunk. Dad helped set up Santa so he wouldn't tip over outside. They figured out how to shine a light on him. I'd never seen Dad so proud of anyone.

I'm not sure what Jack intended to do with Jesus and the Wise Men. I think maybe he wanted to see if they'd show it at the church where he worked lighting candles and carrying plates full of little glasses of wine. Maybe he wanted to give it to

Jane, or to Auntie Irma. But our mother thought it was hers, so she kept it.

METEOR

We learned about falling stars from outer space during the fourth grade. The teacher told us things, and we looked at *Weekly Readers* about the subject. I can't seem to remember what I learned in the classroom, but the display in the hallway made an impression.

While we were in class, somebody came to the hallway and set up tables and poster boards and glass cases about falling stars. There were real meteorites that we could touch, rocks that came from the universe!

Oh, this was nice. I wanted to crawl through my eyes so I could more directly experience these exotic artifacts. Some of the meteorites looked like the rocks in Union Steam Baths, where Dad took me pretty often.

I wondered where the owner of Union Steam Baths got his meteorites. I thought about asking him, but he frightened me. He used to be a boxer. Dad said the owner killed a man when they were boxing. I never wanted to box.

Still, I wondered about those rocks.

I felt the meteorites that we were allowed to touch. I read the names of the places where they were found. How did they land?

Then I saw a framed photograph of a man in a hospital bed, with another smaller picture of something else. I looked closer. In the little picture, it looked like someone's belly—with a piece of it missing. What!

I read the card near the pictures. This man was sleeping when a meteorite crashed through his roof, went right through him, through his bed, and landed on the floor. He didn't die, but oh-my-gosh that meteorite was right there in a case in front of me.

After school, I went straight home. I needed more information. I hoped that Jack would be there. My mother was the only one home.

"What's wrong with you?" she said.

"N-N-Nothing."

"You know I can tell what you're thinking."

I was beginning to doubt that, but I had to get some sentences out.

Very quickly, I told her about meteors and meteorites and the man with a hole in his belly and all the meteorites at the sauna and murder and could meteorites go through our roof and what if I was just walking around outside when one hit me and what is it like to die? And do the meteorites only fall at night?

Grownups must have all this information. There are a lot of saunas with meteorites. I waited.

"There is no such thing. You're making things up again. The Fuller Brush man is coming soon. You need to stay in the basement."

I wished I'd never gone home. Now I was trapped in the basement, in the laundry room. I felt angry. I felt like this was wrong. Jane had told me: "It's bad for her to punish you for asking questions. It could be Evil."

What was I supposed to do? The police wouldn't arrest my mother.

I had recently memorized a prayer to say to remind God about things he needed to do. I heard there were special people called pastors or ministers or priests who were allowed to speak to God about specific things. Maybe one of them could help.

Once, Dad and I sat in the church where Jack worked. A pastor-minister talked, and then sang with other people, and then he talked some more. The specific things he talked about were dead people, sick people, and money.

When Jack worked there, he wore weird clothes and never

smiled. That's why Dad and I were there. Jack wanted us to see him work.

When I walked out of the big room with Dad, the pastor-minister grabbed my hand like older kids did to prove they could beat you up. He smelled like the oil that Grandpa used to put into the special mixture that allowed the outboard motor to make noise and turn the propeller. He also smelled like Uncle Arvi's prune juice and flowers called lilies.

I'm sure that Jack always has a plan, even if it involves working for a smelly bully. But I didn't see how Jack's boss could explain my circumstance to God, let alone get God to help.

Catholic kids said they had a priest. They said he was a nice man who talked to God in front of an audience in their big room.

I asked my mother if we could watch the Catholic priest, but she said no.

"Your Grandpas and Grandmas came from Finland, and that's why we are Lutherans."

I didn't feel like pushing it, even though I knew the truth: Her mother and father were dead, and Dad's mother was Grandma, and she came from Sweden.

I gave up on the God idea.

☯

During the fourth grade I changed what I wanted to be, but not exactly. I decided to be either an archeologist or an anthropologist. I wasn't sure which. I wanted to discover new old-things that people from long ago left in the dirt, like the obsidian arrowhead that I found where a bulldozer dug a place for a parking lot to be built. That would make me an archeologist. I also want to learn about the different ways that people live, whether it's right now, but they're far away, or when it's the past, and they lived anyplace, even right here. That would make me an anthropologist.

I liked fossils, too. Our teacher had fossils that came from dinosaurs. I might find a fossil when I was doing archeology, so that is a factor.

The door at the top of the basement stairs opened. "I'm being set free," I thought.

"Stay down there and keep quiet," my mother growled.

The door closed.

I don't know how it happened. A surge of something, like a really strong feeling, came from my chest into my belly then into my legs. My right knee bent. My foot went back, then...suddenly it all released, and my foot went into the wall. I didn't feel that I was responsible for the hole in the wall, but no one else was there.

When Dad got home, I told him he could whip me for breaking the house he had built. I told him that I had read in a book about the Oregon Trail that dads whipped their sons. I told him that I was afraid that a meteorite might hit me.

Dad got some tools and some wood. He cut back the edges of what he called sheetrock, so the hole I'd made had straight edges. He snuck a piece of wood into the hole and turned screws to keep it there. He got some sheetrock and cut it so it was the same size as the hole. He put glue on the wood in the hole and turned screws through the sheetrock to hold it in place. Dad was really smart, like Jack but different.

Then Dad went into his garage and came back with a little roll of paper and some sweet smelling frosting-like substance. He used a special tool to smooth the frosting-stuff over everything. Soon it looked like the hole I'd kicked had never been there.

"Tomorrow we'll put on another coat," he said, "after this one dries."

I understood.

Several nights later Dad took me to the Upper Field. It was dark and dry. There were a thousand stars or more if you had time to count them. When we both looked above the Little Woods, we saw it: a shooting star.

Dad put his arm around my shoulder.

"Don't worry Pekka," he said. "They'll never get you."

RING THE BELL

I suspected there was something with better flavor than weak Hills Brothers coffee sipped from a metal cup. Still, when experienced outdoors at five in the morning—with Grandpa grinning at the well-prepared trailered boat—Hills Brothers had excellence of its own.

The Jane was a sixteen-foot open wooden boat, set up with two outboard motors—a twenty horse-power and a five horse-power. Grandpa built the heavy boat by himself and named it after my sister. Solid planks, steamed and bent, formed the hull. If cracks developed, Grandpa pounded rope-caulk to fill them. The trim and benches were made from mahogany, coated each year with a foul-smelling amber-tinted liquid.

It was spring. I was ten. Big salmon swarmed in the Columbia River estuary.

We planned to put the boat in at a ramp in Westport, Oregon. From there we'd motor to a sandy beach where the fortunate could catch Chinook salmon. We called it Westport Island.

The coffee in Grandpa's thermos was saturated with sugar.

Brother Jack once heated water in a pan on the stove, adding sugar until it wouldn't take anymore. He poured the liquid into a glass jar where he suspended a metal nut on a string. The next day sugar crystals had formed on the nut and string. I suspected Grandpa's stomach had sugar crystals. He actually stuck a couple more sugar cubes in his mouth before ingesting the already super-sweet drink.

I brought my own thermos.

When we arrived at the boat ramp, there was only one pickup with an empty trailer and nobody in line to launch a boat. Grandpa was happy. He celebrated by shoving a wad of Copenhagen chewing tobacco into his jaw.

Then we heard the sound of a car and boat trailer coming down the gravel road. Grandpa spat out some of his chew and ran to the car. Driving in short bursts back and forth, he jostled the trailer into position. He removed the ties and tossed me a rope that was attached to the bow.

I knew what to do. I jumped onto the dock. Grandpa backed the trailer until the boat floated free. I held the line while Grandpa parked the car. He returned with our thermoses and helped me swing the boat around. He got in the stern and started the twenty-horse. I climbed in at the bow, with the rope.

We slowly left the ramp area as the new arrivals readied their aluminum boat for launch. Grandpa spat some tobacco juice.

We were in a slough with muddy shores where muskrats made their homes. The water was muddy. There were mud-encrusted pilings where log rafts were sometimes tied. Even the air smelled muddy.

Then things changed.

As we came out of the slough into the main stem of the Columbia River, Grandpa cranked the outboard, and the bow of the Jane rose into the fresher air. We rounded a long bend and turned upstream, adjacent to the main channel.

Within a few minutes, we saw the sandy beach where we would claim our spot. Grandpa maneuvered the boat almost perpendicular to the shoreline, gave the motor a rev, and ran the boat into the sand. At the last second, he tipped the top of the motor into the boat, so the propeller missed hitting the sand.

I jumped out with the rope, although it wouldn't be essential to tie off the boat until the tide started coming in. That was the point of getting up early. Grandpa knew that the best time for fishing for spring Chinook was the last part of the ebb tide when the water was as low as it would get. This was technically based on little numbers in a little book called a tide table. But with Grandpa it was subtler than that. He had built-in senses for the tides, the motion of the moon, and the currents of the river.

Looking back toward the slough, we saw the next boat speeding on her way. Grandpa would be nervous until we jammed our pole holders into the sand, providing official notice of our spots for this morning of beach fishing. He placed his holder first, then walked about twenty feet upstream. He motioned back and forth with my holder, giving me the opportunity to fine tune my special spot. This was part of the ritual of luck. I nodded, and he stomped my pole holder in place.

I secured a long rope to the boat with a bowline, then ran up the beach and tied the other end to a log. Grandpa followed to make sure I'd done the job properly.

We fetched our poles and reels from the boat. Grandpa examined his gear, which he had prepared the night before—weight, swivel, leader, Spin-n-Glo. Satisfied, he walked to the edge of the river near his pole holder and cast his gear into the deep water. He let out a little line as he backed up the beach. He placed his pole in the holder and gave the reel a couple of cranks to firm up the line. He removed a cowbell from his pocket and clipped it onto the pole.

He jiggled the pole a bit to demonstrate, for my benefit, the unique sound of his bell. Then he came over to help me with my gear. I had set up a weight and swivel the night before, but I couldn't decide which Spin-n-Glo to use. I had a few in my little tackle box. Grandpa scoffed at the bright pink one and chose his favorite orange and green lure. He called it chartreuse.

When my gear was ready, he motioned for me to cast. It took three attempts before I had placed my gear in an adequate, in his opinion, location. Pole in the holder, I took out my bell. Dad had bought it for me at the sporting goods store downtown. I wanted to go to a real farm to get a real cowbell, but that was out of the question. I don't know why. My bell had a tinny, higher pitched sound. Grandpa liked it because it differed from his.

All the preparations were made. We took our stools and

thermoses from the boat and chose a spot to settle in. It was time for quiet imagination, the telepathic deception that would fool a big salmon into striking at our lures.

Pretty soon, Grandpa's friend John came over to visit. His had been the first boat to make it to the island that morning. He brought his four-legged stool and his thermos. John was a big Finn. Before he sat down, he gathered four tin cans to place under the legs of his stool so it wouldn't sink too far into the sand. Fortunately for John, littering was common in 1963.

Seeing John made me smile inside about a time the previous summer. Grandpa and John sat on the wide front steps at Grandma and Grandpa's house. I was studying the nasturtiums alongside the steps. Dad planted them there when he was a kid.

"Jakko." He called Grandpa by his first name as Grandma did.

"Jakko," John said. "Kun on Fort Chulie."

I perked up. It sounded like John just asked when the Fourth of July was. That was funny. I wondered how Grandpa would handle it. Laugh? Teach?

Grandpa stroked his chin. He replied: "Later part of Yune, first part Yuly."

Better than I hoped!

My reverie was interrupted by loud voices and clanks of metal against metal. The fishermen with the aluminum boat had arrived, just upstream from my pole. Three men noisily prepared their gear. One hadn't even attached his reel to his pole. They passed around a bottle.

Grandpa, John, and I sat and enjoyed our coffees.

After a while, John went to check his gear. I thought I might do the same, but then the bell on the pole upstream from me start ringing. I ran to my pole, unclipped my bell, and reeled in my gear. It was beach fishing etiquette to give your neighbor room to play their fish and bring it in without worrying about getting tied up in someone else's rig.

My neighbor landed a beautiful fish—likely a twenty-pound salmon.

I walked over to congratulate him, but he walked away. Maybe he needs to go to the bathroom, I thought.

I cleaned the crud off of my line and lure. I cast out again. This felt like my best cast ever, but I don't think anyone else noticed.

I returned to our makeshift coffee house. I had just settled back in when my bell rang. My pole bent in a deep curve. Then it snapped back, flinging my bell into the sand. Then the pole bent again.

I ran and grabbed my pole. Grandpa was by my side. He admonished me to keep the tip of the pole up. Line peeled off of my reel; I worried I might run out.

I was able to reel the fish in, but not significantly. The salmon took control. He fought to get into the deeper waters offshore and upstream. It seemed like I was losing more than I could get back.

Grandpa coached, encouraged me. I was having fun, and so was he.

The people with the aluminum boat yelled at us. They wanted Grandpa to take my pole and "horse" the fish in. I noticed that they had not reeled in their gear.

Grandpa told me to stay put and keep the tip of my pole up. He strode over to our neighbors. I don't know what he said, but two of them immediately pulled in their gear. The third handed Grandpa the bottle they had passed around earlier.

My fish jumped. Oh my goodness this was a big salmon. It rolled to give me another look at its heft. Then it dove. Line squealed off my reel.

I worked that fish for over twenty minutes.

In the end, I brought him close enough that Grandpa could encircle him with the big landing net. Grandpa fell as he dragged the netted fish ashore. I was exposed to some colorful Finnish curses. We had a thirty-pound Spring Chinook.

That was enough. The day was not going to get warm enough to dry Grandpa's clothes. John offered to build a fire, but Grandpa declined. He offered John the bottle that he had purloined from the noisy neighbors. John didn't want it, so they dumped the liquid out.

"Hyvä kala, Pekka," said Grandpa. Good fish. Together, we lifted the salmon, put it in the fish box, and carefully packed ice around it.

STUTTER

My mother was the only one home. Even though I knew she didn't appreciate such things I just had to tell someone—anyone, a cat—about mathematics and my new abilities.

"You think too much," she said. My mother often said that, like it was something she was required to recite.

Why? I paused to think about what she meant. Did she mean that I had a sickness, like the measles, that was caused by thinking? That didn't make sense. I used thoughts, that were part of thinking, like a slice of bread was part of a loaf, to figure things out. I could think about two numbers and add them to get one answer or subtract one from the other to get another answer. It depended on the sign—or the story problem.

Last year when the fourth grade was almost over we practiced multiplication. There were tables with answers, but I wasn't sure that the tables could be trusted. They left important stuff out, especially negative numbers.

When I went to the library, I easily found books with negative numbers and other wonderful things like square roots and equations. On my figuring paper I drew a square root sign with a negative one inside, then the equals sign, then i. Below that, I wrote: i times i equals -1. I felt happy about this, my first imaginary number.

I quietly told Mrs. Nance, our teacher, about negative numbers. She was nice and really smart about rocks and dinosaurs. I thought she would be glad that I had discovered that the multiplication tables needed to get fixed. I showed her my figuring sheet. I asked if she thought we should include imaginary numbers such as i or just negative numbers for now. She asked if she could show my figuring sheet to someone.

The next day I was called out of class to go to a room with Mr. Reuter, who was from the high school. He knew about imaginary numbers, and he had books with lots of equations. He knew Jack!

Two times a week until the end of the school year he came to visit me. We talked about and did mathematics. It was fun.

Now it was the start of the fifth grade. Mr. Reuter wanted to meet some more, but the only time he could come to Captain Robert Gray school was at the same time when I was supposed to go to Speech Therapy.

"Why do you go there?" he asked.

"Because I stutter."

"I've never heard you stutter."

"Sure you have. I do it all the time." I heard what I just said. What's going on?

"Maybe you got over it."

"This is strange. I'm not even trying. I don't even have marbles in my mouth."

"What?"

"Maybe it's mathematics."

Mr. Reuter took me to the school office. He told the secretary and another lady about mathematics and Speech Therapy. They seemed confused. The principal who hits kids with his paddle came in. Was I in trouble? I didn't feel scared. The principal said they should see if they could get me not to stutter. He talked like I wasn't there.

"What would you like for me to say?" They all stared at me like I was a teddy bear come to life. "I could try reading out loud. I have a science book right here."

No one said anything, so I read. I read a paragraph about how sugar dissolves into water. I noticed an error in the book and started to explain, but Mr. Reuter gave me a little shake of the head, so I stopped talking. I was excited, but I made a poker face.

The secretary and principal went into the principal's office, and they closed the door. A short while later they came out. The secretary typed on a stack of papers that already had words. She used carbon papers. She put two of the papers and one carbon paper in an envelope. She gave it to me and said that Dad or my mother had to sign the paper so I could learn from Mr. Reuter, who right then had the biggest smile.

☯

"Do you hear what I'm not doing?" I said.

No reaction.

"Here's a hint: I'm not stuttering."

My mother was about to say her sentence against thinking, again.

I ran for the kitchen door. I was getting out of there. I knew her voice was about to change. As I closed the door behind me, I heard a shrill cackle:

"You think too much."

I ran down the trail, across the field, and didn't slow down until I got to Auntie Irma's house.

I was surprised to see Dad's pickup there. He came out of the house, smiling.

"Mr. Reuter called me," said Dad.

Jack was there, too!

I demonstrated non-stuttering until after it got dark. No one asked me to stop.

CHAPTER THREE

FAMILY

HIGH TIDE

I didn't expect to learn about using grappling hooks to find a body—ever, certainly not on a dark January night when I had just turned twelve.

Dad and I watched a surprising winter sunset from the end of Pier Two, at the Port of Astoria docks. Lately, we'd parked on that pier just about every day. I loved it.

Sometimes we'd hear crew members from the ships speaking Japanese or other languages. If we were lucky to be there when a ship had just docked, we could witness long lines of huge rats run down the thick mooring ropes.

Often we watched the longshoremen work on massive log rafts. They'd snag a log with a twelve-foot pole that had a hook and prodder on the end. They guided the log onto a looped braided steel cable fed out from a crane. Sometimes they fixed a loop on the log so a hook on the end of the cable could grab it. A man in a boxlike area high up guided the end of the crane and the cable. He pulled the logs up and onto a ship. I was always amazed that the logs ended up neatly piled high on the ships.

It sure looked challenging to be on those log rafts, standing on floating, shifting logs while other logs and that heavy cable swung in the air. I'd seen a log accidentally slip out of the cable and fall in the river. The wake made the log raft undulate wildly. Longshoremen braced themselves with their poles. I expect they were grateful to be wearing their special boots with sharp metal grips. I heard they sometimes died, but I never saw it happen.

After sundown, the Columbia River looked deeper than in daylight. The river was about four miles wide at the near point in Washington, where the ferries landed. When I looked straight at the mouth of the river, I realized that there was nothing but water all the way to Japan.

I sure was lucky, I thought…but my thought was interrupted.

A horn sounded. A pickup moved fast between the high piles of lumber on Pier Two. Soon it was right beside us.

"George," the guy said to Dad, breathless. "Urho fall offa the dock dare atta Seven Street. Ve gotta hook 'im for tide turn. Can you go getta more grapplery from shipyard?"

"I'll go. Are there enough boats?"

"Plenty boats. Ve needa more hook."

Dad started his pickup, swung around and drove up to Marine Drive. Only then did he seem to notice I was there.

"You'll have to come with me."

I suppose.

He turned right on Marine Drive and accelerated past Smith Point, where the East end of Youngs Bay meets the Columbia River. The currents there were dangerous. I knew…

"We're going to Bumble Bee Shipyard to get some grappling hooks. I need you to help carry a few ropes. We need to move fast. Are you okay?"

"What are grappling hooks?"

Dad had dodged my nascent pubescent questions by sending me to the library or to my brother Jack. This one he would have to take on himself.

"Big hooks. Haven't you seen them? We're going to use them to hook Urho."

"Won't that hurt him?"

"The fall off Seventh Street probably killed him. If not, the water is so cold he would die fast."

"Why are we doing this if he's already dead?"

Dad looked perplexed and frantic at the same time. He turned at the entrance to Bumble Bee Shipyard.

"If we don't find him, his family won't have his body to put in a casket."

This brought up a whole lot of other questions, but I realized it was time to act.

The security guard had got a phone call that someone would be coming. "Do you know where they are?"

"Yes. Come on, Peter."

Dad ran toward the place where they keep the bandsaw blades. Hung on round extensions from the high wall, they must have been twenty feet long. Jack showed them to me last year. He said they were for cutting the big timbers that they needed for ships. Jack knew a lot about this place where everything was giant-sized, but I don't think he liked it any more than I did.

There they were: the grappling hooks. I imagined that they might be something like gigantic versions of the three-way hooks we used for catching salmon. Pretty close. Had I seen one before?

"Okay, Peter," Dad said to me, giving me a look that said that he didn't mean to put me in this situation when I was still in the low double-digits of age, but he expected that I could handle it. "Pick up as many of these coils of rope as you can carry and still walk fast back to the truck."

For his part, Dad carefully scooped up ten grappling hooks. Half had coils of rope already attached.

I gathered six coils and decided that was my limit.

"Leave one of those here. Let's go!"

Soon we were flying by Smith Point. I wanted to tell Dad what I had done at Smith Point but now was not for talking.

We drove to the waterfront past the port, over by the big cannery. There were a lot of men with lanterns and flashlights. The man Dad talked with at Pier Two was there.

"Take the ones with ropes and get them to the boats." Dad sounded like he was taking charge.

"Peter. You know a bowline," he told me. "Let's set up the rest."

He grabbed a rope and a grappling hook. I did the same. He rigged three. I rigged two. He checked my knots, then ran to talk to some men. They followed him back to the pickup.

“I don’t know how long this will take. Stay in the truck, Peter.”

A couple of men took the grappling hook setups and climbed down to the boats. Dad paused before following. It was like he was sniffing the air to feel the currents of the river. That’s what I thought. Then he went to the boats.

I waited all of a few minutes before I moved in for a closer look. Some of the boats were roped together. Some were tied to one or more of the dozens of piling under the cannery complex.

While it was still in the slack high tide, the flow of the river was almost gentle in the shallows near the shore. Urho’s body might be hung up on a piling or other support structures. This was the most likely place to find him. How did I know this stuff?

I could see Dad on one of the boats further out, throwing and retrieving the hook.

I sure didn’t want to be in Urho’s situation.

Last summer I got into some trouble with that river. I liked to play along the shore of Youngs Bay, near Smith Point. Logs and planks and all sorts of things washed ashore there.

I decided to make a raft.

It took a couple of weeks before I decided my craft was seaworthy, but when that day came, I was ready to go. I had a special pole that I thought would be good for navigating. I used it to shove my raft loose from the shore—with me aboard

The raft floated fine, but my special pole was useless. I picked up speed heading toward Smith Point. I could tell that the current got really fast on the river side of the Point. It would probably send me all the way to the ocean. I jumped off and swam to shore. When I was safe, I looked for my raft. It was headed toward Warrenton.

☯

Men shouted; lights moved in different directions. Boats were untied to make room... I tried to spot Dad.

There appeared to be a body on a tarp on a gillnet boat

coming to shore. My eyes wouldn't blink.

Dad tapped me on the shoulder. I jumped in the air, my hair stood up, and my belly got rearranged all at the same time. I turned around and hugged Dad.

"Have you ever done this before?" I asked.

"A few times. Don't you remember?"

"Remember what?"

"You were with me last time. A few years ago."

"What grade was I in? How old was I?"

"I think you were six or seven."

I did not remember. I could remember six pretty well and seven even better. There were a lot of blank spots. Everyone had blank spots. For example, that's where we put secrets.

"No. I don't remember. I was a kid."

Dad laughed. "You're still a kid. Let's get some coffee over there." He gestured toward a table with a lantern and a camp stove. The recovery workers were getting warm.

He had coffee. I had hot chocolate, with marshmallows.

I told Dad what I had done at Smith Point. His eyes got wide as I told him about jumping off the raft.

"Peter, I did the very same thing, at the very same place, when I was a kid."

I felt happiness inside. I hoped and hoped that sometime soon Dad and I would build a boat together.

SLIDE RULE

"What's that?" I asked Jack. He was at his desk fiddling with a white thing that looked like a ruler with lots of extra numbers. When I first saw it, a warm and happy feeling flowed inside my chest.

"It's a slide rule," said Jack. "This device makes it easier to figure out the answer to a problem."

The word "problem" made my thoughts race away on a tangent. Problem was what some people said my mother had. My mother said I was a problem child. I could read and spell the word before I became five, but I was confused about what it meant.

"...or a cosign or a tangent." Jack was explaining about the super ruler, but I hadn't listened to what he said. I had heard Jack's words, but I didn't place attention on them. Instead, I had gone on a tangent. Jane taught me about tangents. She said they are like imaginary vacations. Sometimes you like them, sometimes you wish you had stayed home.

"How did you know that I was on a tangent?"

Jack smiled. He said, "Tangent can have different meanings. You could be on a tangent when you talk about something that doesn't have anything to do with the conversation. Or a tangent might send you on a daydream. A tangent is also a part of trigonometry, which is a way of applying multiplication and division to geometry." He looked pleased that he got all that out at once.

"I was having a day thought, or more like a lot of thoughts all strung together," I confessed.

"That could be a tangent, but my meaning had to do with

trigonometry."

Jack was inspired to draw a triangle. He put "angle" near one of the points. Then he put "opposite" by one line, "adjacent" by another line, and "hypotenuse" by the longest line. Then he wrote, "tangent equals" followed by "opposite" with a line below it. Below the line, he wrote "adjacent."

"If we knew what the numbers were for some of this we could figure out the rest by multiplying or dividing," Jack explained.

It looked like fun, but I didn't understand. "What about the super ruler?"

"Oh yeah," said Jack, "I got off on a tangent." He laughed at his own joke. I didn't get it in time to catch a laugh.

"Anyway, the slide rule gives us the answers." He showed me some simple multiplication and division. Wow. My tummy joined my chest in happy movement.

"Where do we keep these slide rules?" They had to be the most important things that grownups had, except maybe houses, cars, and refrigerators.

"This is the only one. They bought it for me to use in trigonometry class."

"Does Jane have one?"

"No."

"Why not?"

"Because I'm probably going to be an engineer and Jane is not."

"What does an engineer do?"

"There are different types of engineers. Mostly they're men."

"Why?"

"Because different things need engineering."

"I meant why are engineers men? Is it because it is dangerous to work on trains?"

"That's a different type of engineer. Mathematical expert engineers are men because the government thinks that men are better at math than women."

“Is that true? And how can the government think? It’s not even an animal.”

Dad called us from down the hall. “Let’s go to Irma and Arvi’s.”

We were happy to go to our aunt and uncle’s house.

I asked Jack, “Will you bring your sliding ruler?”

“Okay,” said Jack. “Slide rule.”

SEEING STARS

A powerful blow to the side of my head knocked me to the gymnasium floor. I saw the basketball coming with my corner-eye vision, just before impact.

Cartoon characters on TV get walloped in the head, and their heads turn to stars. Now I knew how that felt. I was surprised. I was confused. I couldn't get up right away. The whole side of my head hurt.

I looked in the direction that the ball came from. I thought that some kids were playing and I accidentally got hit. The gym was packed with fifth and sixth graders at recess. I should have been more alert.

Then I saw Randy laughing. Celebrating. Looking right at me. He had deliberately thrown the ball as hard as he could, intending to hit me in the head. A sensation seethed through my body. Anger.

I averted my eyes from Randy, knowing that would deny part of his pleasure. I got up and left the gym.

Hours later, I still felt anger toward Randy. Even when I went to bed, I felt the same, maybe more, anger. I thought about times I'd seen other kids hurt by Randy—shoved, slapped, tripped… He was the biggest kid in the fifth grade. And he was mean.

I had heard that there was something wrong with Randy. He'd been held back in school. He was older; that's why he was bigger. I remembered my mother told me to be nice to Randy because he had a disease. How did she know that? Did she have the same disease?

When I woke up, the anger boiled again. This was new. It

was like I needed the anger to prevent a terrible feeling in my belly. I wanted to hurt Randy.

I wanted revenge, but it wasn't so simple. I had never deliberately hurt anyone. I learned at Sunday school that Jesus said if somebody hits you on one side of your face you should offer to let them hit the other side. I wasn't going to do that.

I knew that Pete Seeger, and Peter, Paul and Mary, and Joan Baez, and Henry David Thoreau believed war was a bad way to solve problems. My brother, Jack, told me.

I was confused. Dad had gone to a war on a destroyer and killed people in airplanes they were trying to crash into his ship.

There were people who were so mad at other people that they would plan ahead to put gas in their airplanes and go out to find a destroyer to crash into. I asked Dad about this.

"And bombs," he said.

"What?"

"They had bombs in the planes."

"Why didn't they just drop the bombs on you and fly away?"

"They thought it would scare us more if they showed us that they were so crazy that they would die to kill us. They really wanted to sink the aircraft carriers."

I nodded. Dad didn't like talking about this.

"Destroyers were there to protect the carriers. I shot the planes down with a five-inch gun."

"But why were they so mad?"

"They were brainwashed by an emperor who wanted to rule the world with Hitler."

I was full of whys. Dad had explained this before.

"They were enemies." He made a long pause after 'enemies.' "If we didn't get them, they would get us. You wouldn't be here."

When he got to this point, I could always feel his sadness. He didn't know the guy in the plane. But he killed him. Dad never said that, but I could feel it.

This talk helped me, even if Dad didn't know it.

If Randy didn't stop hurting kids, someone might die. I didn't want him to be my enemy. I didn't want to kill him. But something had to happen. This boiling anger meant something.

Randy was too big for me to fight. I didn't know how to fight anyway. I'd seen other kids have fights, but it was never something I wanted to do. I wondered if Randy picked on kids he knew wouldn't hit him. That was me. Or was it? Then it came to me.

On *Death Valley Days*, pretty often cowboys or outlaws or Indians hid behind rocks or trees and surprise-attacked the people they had been arguing with. That way they could win even if there were fewer of the hiding ones, or if they didn't have as good weapons.

I would surprise Randy and surprise him good.

In *Outdoor Life* magazine I saw pictures of how to catch anything from a rabbit to a wolf by digging a hole and hiding it with thin branches. Hunters would wait until the animal stepped on the branches and fell into the hole. Then they could clobber the animal. My animal would be Randy.

I selected a spot hidden by the big spruce tree off the trail to school. For over a week, a couple hours each day, I dug the hole. I used a shovel and a hatchet for the roots. I'd camouflage the hole when I was done for the day. Finally, when the hole was big enough and a little more, I placed the thin branches I'd gathered and added some leaves.

In *Outdoor Life* some hunters stood up sharpened spears in their hole so the animal would be impaled and easier to kill. I didn't plan on killing Randy, so I omitted that part.

Now to lure my prey.

After school, I asked Randy if he wanted to walk with me. That was his first surprise because I had always avoided him. I said, "I have something neat to show you."

We walked up the path. I pointed at the spruce tree.

"You can go first."

That was his second surprise. Nobody was nice to him.

Almost time for the third surprise. Just a little bit further...

"Where is it?" he said.

"Lean that way."

I could tell he was off balance. I pushed him onto the branches and down into the hole. I jumped in and pummeled him with my fists.

He didn't even fight back. He cried.

I explained to Randy that worse things will happen to him if he ever hurt me or any of the long list of friends that I recited.

"Get it?" I demanded.

"Yes," he sobbed.

He ran home crying. I wished he didn't have to cry. The anger I had toward him was gone. He seemed smaller.

I hid out in the Little Woods until Dad got home. My mother would probably take a side against me when Randy's parents called.

When Dad drove his pickup down the driveway, I came running. I told him what I had done. I even showed him the hole.

"You did what you had to do, Peter," he said. "You're not in trouble. But don't think every problem can be solved like this."

I stayed outside. My mother yelled at Dad for a long time.

MOTHBALLED

Auntie Irma had mothballs in her closets. I'd smelled them. It wasn't a good smell.

"Why don't you put perfume in your closet?" I asked, explaining, "I'm doing some research."

"That's an interesting idea," said Auntie Irma, smiling. "I guess partly because I like different perfumes at different times and sometimes none at all. Also, somebody might come to visit and hang up their coat. What if they didn't like the perfume…"

I could tell that she was getting warmed up to talk for a long time. "Does anyone like the smell of mothballs?"

"Well, no. Why?"

"Because you have mothballs in your closet."

"Those are for the moths."

I laughed. "The moths like the way they smell?"

"The moths don't like the smell. They stay away, instead of laying eggs."

"Why don't we eat their eggs?"

Auntie Irma made a funny face. "They're not good to eat. When they hatch they turn into worms—Peter, let me finish. No, not fishing worms—little worms that eat wool."

"Like wool blankets." And coats. This was starting to make sense.

"They'll eat holes in our clothes. I don't like the smell, but it works to keep the moths away."

"Thank you."

Dad had his uniform from the Navy. It was wool. There are hundreds and thousands of men who used to wear wool uniforms. Some men need a place to keep their uniforms. Why not on an old ship?

The next day, as planned, Dad took Jack and me to the place where the Navy Liberty ships were mothballed. He wanted the three of us to fish for sturgeon. We borrowed Grandpa's boat, the Jane.

The Army Corps of Engineers had dug a big deep hole in the river for the Navy to put ships that they didn't need anymore as well as mothballs and uniforms because now we have liberty. That wasn't hard to figure out.

Grandpa wouldn't fish for sturgeon. He wouldn't eat them. He thought that they lived on the bottom of the river and ate what he called "plooshon." He believed that poop and fallout and mercury and chemicals were in the muck of the deepest parts of the river.

I wasn't so sure about the sturgeon either. They reminded me of Ichthyosaur. But I liked fishing.

We launched the boat and Dad took us right into the middle of the anchored mothball ships. They were tall. They were rusty. They were spooky. Among them, even in the middle of the day, it seemed dark.

I tried to sniff for mothballs, but I couldn't catch the scent. I hoped it would remain that way.

We got our fishing gear together: stout poles, thick line, herring with hooks hid inside them, lead weights, and leather pole holders to strap on if we hooked a big sturgeon. They could get big, not as big as Ichthyosaur, but over ten feet. I heard they could get to twenty-five feet. What would we do if we caught a giant one? The boat is only sixteen feet...

I caught a sturgeon right away. It was strong, but it didn't seem that big. I pulled it right in with the heavy gear. It was almost three feet long. Dad said it was too small, so we put it back. Fine with me. I loved dinosaurs, and I didn't want to kill a fish that reminded me of them.

After we put mine back, it seemed like we couldn't get a bite. Maybe the sturgeon have a fishermen warning system, like the bees that tell other bees where they find flowers. The bees dance to talk. Do sturgeons do a swimming dance? I didn't let on what I was thinking. I was secretly on the sturgeon's side, while Dad wanted to eat one.

Then I remembered something.

President Kennedy visited Tongue Point, right over by where we'd launched the boat, last year before he was murdered in Dallas. Sometime before that, I heard him say on TV he wanted to "Get America Moving Again." Jack told me that meant the President wanted to have more missiles than the Russians.

I hadn't seen a missile. They fly without the big wings that airplanes need. They carry atom bombs. The bombs use radiation made upstream on the Columbia River, past The Dalles, at Hanford.

I remembered about a Finnish whale with radiation. Older kids talked about it. Fishermen killed it in the ocean by Depoe Bay. Did Jack know about this?

Of course, he did. Jack explained that, first, it wasn't a Finnish whale; it was a Fin whale.

"That doesn't help."

"It's named after its flippers, not after the country."

"Oh. Did it go all the way to Hanford to get radiation?"

"No. Have you seen the dams?"

"I've seen Bonneville and The Dalles."

"This whale was 55-feet long."

I thought about the fish ladders at Bonneville. It wouldn't fit. "So, how did it get the radiation?"

"They think it was something it ate."

"It ate radiation?"

"More likely it ate something that ate radiation that was in something it ate."

"How did the fishermen even discover the radiation?"

"They didn't. A scientist from the government thought this could happen, so he bought part of the whale. Something like that."

"So Grandpa is right."

"Right about...What the heck!" Jack's pole bent. It almost jumped out of the boat.

"Hold the pole up," shouted Dad. He shifted the outboard motor into neutral and leaned toward Jack with one of the leather holders.

Jack's pole was bent in a half-circle, and it was a thick, solid pole. His reel whined as the line pulled off. Maybe he caught a submarine?

Then I remembered how big sturgeon could get. I reeled in my line as quick as I could.

Dad and Jack maneuvered the pole holder around Jack's waist. The fish was still taking line. Jack was more relaxed wearing the pole holder.

Dad shifted the motor to go. He began to follow the fish. He'd done this before, I was certain. A moment later and we were all laughing, even though nobody had told a joke.

Jack's pole straightened out. He swiftly reeled in the slack line.

"Do you still have him?" Dad shouted. He slowed the motor as we neared the side of a mothball ship.

"I don't know." Jack was almost crying. Why? Did a big fish mean that much to him?

Jack's pole bent again. The reel squealed. He still had the fish.

It went on like this for it seemed like an hour. Realistically, I thought, what if we get this fish beside the boat? What would we do? I guess if it's not too huge I could lasso it and we could drag it to the boat landing.

It seemed like Jack had lost more line than he reeled back in.

Dad looked at his watch. Jack noticed and looked at his, too. What's going on?

"We're going to have to cut the line," said Dad.

"Why!" I yelled.

Jack said, "I have play practice. Remember? 'The Diary of Anne Frank.'"

No, I didn't remember. And what could be more important than at least trying to help Jack land this fish? What could be more important than the three of us together?

Jack did it himself. Before I could finish thinking, he pulled out his sharp pocket knife, opened the blade one-handed, tightened the drag on his reel, and cut the line near the reel-feed.

About thirty feet ahead a huge sturgeon rolled. It was at least nine feet long.

JANE KRISTINE

The old wood-frame building shook and swayed. I put my coffee cup neatly on its saucer. It rattled. My sister Jane did the same with her cup, but now it sounded like dozens of cups and saucers rattling.

We sat side-by-side on her sofa in a small room. Across from us was a tall, wide glass-fronted display case. Jane collected milk glass. I have no idea why. She arranged her collection and other treasures in this impractical case that required too much dusting, in my opinion.

"It's an earthquake. I know it's an earthquake. Just like last year in Alaska," I thought. In my mind was every picture that I'd ever seen of the 1964 quake that swallowed houses and sent big waves all the way to California.

I thought about running to Jane's stairs, but I imagined them all discombobulated like the stairs in that tall book about a house with lots of rooms.

I wondered if Jane had an idea about what to do. I glanced her way. She was leaning forward like a cat preparing to pounce. I looked at the display case. It was starting to fall toward us.

I had heard about calculus. If I knew the right equations, I could solve the problem mathematically. I would need to know details about the mass of the display case and the objects, about factors that resist and accelerate movement, about the intensity and speed of the earthquake, about the thickness of the glass and...when it would hit our bodies!

There were probably other things that I would need to know if I was to complete my equation, but that last one was pretty important. Unless we changed the probabilities vastly, I might never properly learn the equations of calculus, let alone those of probability and statistics.

Jane gave me a slight nod and—like magic—we were both on our feet leaning forward with our hands flat on the glass front of the case, varying pressure perfectly, without even designing an equation. There we rode out the quake.

Not one of her collectibles was damaged.

Our coffee had spilled. Jane got a towel to clean up the mess. I got more coffee from the pot on the stove.

We sat back down and looked at the case. We looked at each other. I spoke. "Have you ever tried stamp collecting?"

☯

Jane was a discoverer. She found new things, new ways to think, and new ways to feel about the universe and its people. She was wise.

She was also beautiful. She was dramatically beautiful like when she put on a wonderful white outfit to play an angel. Auntie Irma made the outfit and helped Jane with her halo.

I bowed to her and laughed. She chased me away.

She was also beautiful in pants and a sweatshirt. She and her boyfriend, the drummer, once took me to the Euphoria coffeehouse, across the bridge to Miles Crossing. People there had bongos. They talked about different ways to think. I didn't tell anyone I was a poet because I was afraid they would expect me to slap a bongo while I told a rhyme. Jane kept my cover.

Jane discovered new foods. Because we were Finns, our mother cooked the right foods for Finns: meatballs, pasty, chuck steak, soft peas, cream-style corn, hard tack, butter, mashed potatoes, limpu. And salmon, smelt, and razor clams whenever we could get them.

Although Jane was okay with most of the Finn foods; at her house, she added zucchini, cabbage, Wonder bread, beef stroganoff, and more. Some I liked, including German Chocolate cake; others, I didn't, particularly zucchini casserole with tomatoes.

I tried everything, even if I had to spit it out.

☯

Jane wanted to help me with my difficulties.

"Out with it," she said. "Tell me what's going on."

With Jack at college and Jane in her apartment, I thought that they were safe from getting murdered, but my feelings did not agree.

"Nothing."

She looked at my eyes and grabbed my shoulder like she was going to shake me. She wanted to shake my secrets out and stop more from forming. I could feel her wanting in my chest and in my belly. There was no way I could allow her to know the secrets. If I told, she would die.

"Someday we need to make a plan. You are so smart."

"Not so smart with a basketball," I suggested, desperate to change the subject.

Jane was the only family that came to my sixth-grade basketball game when Captain Robert Gray played against John Jacob Astor.

The teams came out from our halftime rest. I was the small forward. We gathered around the center of the court. The referee threw the ball straight up. The tallest guy from each team tried to slap the ball to a teammate.

I got the ball!

I ran. I dribbled. I went in for a layup. The crowd was making noise.

I missed the shot. That's okay. I got my own rebound. I banked the ball off the backboard. I missed. The crowd yelled. I got the rebound again!

Then I saw the referee walking toward me. My teammates were standing in the middle of the court. A lot of people in the audience were laughing.

I'd forgotten that we change baskets after the break. I felt terrible.

Jane ran right out onto the court and hugged me.

I reminded her about that time. She smiled. And she tickled me.

☯

Jane went to Lewis and Clark College. She was super smart.

Jane wrote a special feature for the newspaper about women in business. She interviewed women in Clatsop County and some in Pacific County, Washington, too. She told stories about flower shops, fish markets, restaurants, an upholsterer and more—all businesses owned and run by women.

Jane always had books to loan me, and suggestions for books I would enjoy. She was almost always right about what I would like.

One time she said I should read *One Flew Over the Cuckoo's Nest*, and *I Never Promised You a Rose Garden*, and *Tender is the Night*.

They were good books, but I wouldn't recommend reading them one after the other. I said that to Jane, and she showed me the stack of books she was reading. I scanned them. Every one of the books included people who either had mental confusion, emotions that they didn't want, or the impression they were someone else—or many someones else.

Jane sometimes had grand mal seizures. She would shake like she had her own personal earthquake inside. After she stopped, she would be silent and tired. I would be, too, if I shook like that.

Jane saw visions.

When the visions came, I tried to protect her. Everyone else thought there was something wrong about what she said and did. Why couldn't they see that she was a discoverer? Maybe she needed to explore a special place with different rules and customs?

QUARTZ LAKE

Dad loved to drive on logging roads. You didn't need to be a logger to drive on them, although Dad could be an honorary logger because he worked with the wood that was logged. He made houses and cabinets and boats.

Usually, Dad took Jack on the logging road drives. The roads were gravel and sometimes just dirt, and you needed a truck or a jeep to follow them. Dad's pickup had a bench seat, and it was hard to shift gears if someone was sitting in the middle. Lately, though, I got to go with them.

One time, the three of us went camping and got to where we camped by driving on the logging roads. I wondered how Dad knew the way. In Clatsop County, there were hundreds of miles of logging roads. There were mainlines and spurs and everything in between. There weren't signs, just occasional flat sticks with a couple of numbers. We didn't have a map.

"How do you know how to get there?" I asked.

Dad smiled. He said, "An old, old man who lives in the forest taught me how to make a picture in my mind. I allow all of the views I've ever seen of these woods and roads to gather together to build a big picture. It's like looking down from an airplane, except that I can zoom in." He touched his forehead then reached toward the windshield.

Jack nudged me and said, "BS."

"Your brother doesn't believe me now," Dad continued, "but one day both of you will know The Way of the Lay of the Land."

Dad stopped the pickup and put it in reverse. I protected my nose from getting hit by his elbow, narrowly.

"I almost missed a cross-over," Dad explained.

After about three hours of driving, and a lot of different roads, we came to a lake. Dad enjoyed a cigarette. Jack ran down to the water. I was happy to get out of the middle seat.

"Peter," hollered Jack. "Come see this."

I walked down to the lakeshore and looked where Jack pointed. At first, the sun played on the water so I couldn't see beneath the surface. I moved to a slightly different spot. There were dozens of western newts cavorting in the crystal clear water. At any moment, some would pop their snouts into the air for a breath, while others dived deep. Still others swam around in circles.

Amphibians were my favorite animal type. They spend part of their lives in water and part on land. Newts are amphibians.

Western newts are brown on top and yellow-orange on the bottom. When they're on land, the brown color helps them blend in with the dirt, so it's harder for raccoons and bobcats to see, catch, and eat them. In the water, I supposed, the light color camouflaged them from fish hunting from below. But I might have it wrong. Since the newts are poisonous to people, I expect they're poisonous to some other animals as well. They contain the poison tetrodotoxin.

"Have you ever seen anything like it?" Jack was excited. "Look how big it is."

Jack was not referring to the newts. I moved closer to him.

"That's the biggest piece of quartz I've ever seen," he said.

Sunlight entered the lake and played off the facets of the huge underwater quartz construct. The amazing mineral formation split the light into bedazzling colors.

"Come on." Dad was pulling stuff out of the open bed of the pickup. "Let's pitch the tent."

☯

Western newts interested me, not only for being poisonous amphibians but also because they have a sort of a third eye. Their third eye can sense light and dark. It's connected to their pineal gland.

People have a pineal gland, as well, but ours is in the middle of our brains. The neurotransmitter serotonin produces melatonin in the pineal gland. Melatonin, among other things, helps balance our rhythms of sleep and wakefulness.

Only a few months before this camping trip, I completed my sixth-grade science project which was about the pineal gland—the organ that Rene Descartes considered both the seat of the soul and the place where thoughts are formed.

I didn't agree or disagree with Descartes. But he had made the pineal gland famous, so that probably encouraged interest in my project.

My project was mostly about providing as much information as possible about the pineal gland, with references to scientific papers. I suggested some ideas for experiments, such as giving amphibians small doses of melatonin over some time and observing any changes relative to a control group. I also suggested experiments that involved removing the pineal surface structure from amphibians with an obvious "third eye."

The judges thought that my project was good. They gave me gold stickers and an abstract trophy. Best of all, I got a scholarship to summer science camp, where I studied nearshore ocean ecosystems, extracted and preserved fossils, and met an owl named Owl.

I liked to draw biochemical molecules and to compare the ways their connections play out in larger structures. I was fascinated to notice remarkable similarities between serotonin and psilocybin. This suggested a relationship with another of my interests—human consciousness. Someday I might create an experiment...

Jane came to the science fair and spent a lot of time with my project. Later that week, I went to her apartment. She liked the information about hormones that I had presented. She told me about farmers who give hormones to chickens to make them grow faster.

"What if you gave growth hormones to a fully grown animal?" I suggested. "Maybe they'd jump to the next stage of evolution."

Jane laughed. "What if there was a hormone that made people nicer?"

I tried, "What if there was a hormone that made people jump to a new level of consciousness?"

Jane said, "Who would know?"

We both laughed.

In her refrigerator, Jane had chicken drumsticks she had fried the day before. We ate them.

☯

The camp was set. Jack had designed and built a kitchen made from rocks and fallen tree limbs, with a perfect spot for our four-burner Coleman cookstove.

Dad placed his folding chair in a sunny spot and grabbed a beer from the big cooler. He suggested, "How about you two catch some fish?"

Jack had no interest in fishing. He wanted to explore. There were no obvious trails, but that wasn't a problem. I recalled the time we ran down Saddle Mountain, completely ignoring the trail system.

We discovered several boulders. Jack ran back to the truck and grabbed a crowbar Dad had stashed behind the seat. He ran at a boulder as if he was attacking it. He almost fell on his face.

I checked out one of the smaller boulders. This one had a crack that appeared to almost break it into two pieces.

"Try the crowbar here," I said.

Jack stuck the crowbar into the crack and leaned his weight into it. The boulder separated, one portion almost landing on my foot.

It was quartz.

"How did these get here?" I said, quick with the unnecessary question.

Jack was in his pondering mode. He might have a detailed earth-science lesson ready to go, or he might make something up.

"I don't know," he answered.

"Don't you even have a ridiculous guess?"

"As it retreated, the last glacier of the last ice age dropped a bunch of quartz boulders over this part of the Coast Range. Then, 10,000 years ago, two tribes of Bigfoot had a war. The tribe that won got to demand that the losers move all the quartz boulders here, to build a lake. The lake was only partly built when word was passed up to the Bigfoot at the lake that peace had been achieved among all the Bigfoot tribes. The Bigfoot left the boulders where we found them today."

"That's more like it." I clapped.

☯

I had a fly rod with a floating line and a small elegant fly. I neatly dropped the fly over a deep hole. I got a strike right away. Then I got another. Then I realized what was happening: western newts were hitting on my fly.

Jack set up his fly fishing outfit. He chose a large fly that I had tied. It was one of my first efforts. I tried to talk Jack out of using the monstrosity, but he wouldn't listen.

Jack's line floated along the shoreline. With wrist action, he rolled his line, plonking the hideous fly into a new location.

I saw the shadow rise and encase the fly. Jack had a fish on. Jack let the fish play, then moved it close to shore. I dampened a small net in the lake water and got ready to scoop up the trout.

"Give it to me," Jack commanded. "I want to dip-net my own fish."

I complied. Jack brought in an eighteen-inch trout.

My brother seemed happy, so we repeated the process. Before long, Jack had the twin of his first fish. That was all we needed.

I cleaned the fish. Jack fried them on the Coleman.

Dad asked us how the walk around the lake went. Jack responded with a version of his Bigfoot story.

"That's BS," said Dad.

CHAPTER FOUR

FLIGHT

DUKE

I had the happenstance of a brief encounter with one of America's great composers, even though I didn't recognize him at the time.

Aunt Helen, Uncle Bill, and I were on our way to Helsinki. We planned to spend most of the summer of 1967 in Scandinavia. They thought that it might be fun to stop over for a few days in New York City. It was.

When I turned thirteen, during my seventh grade in school, I had no idea that I would soon be visiting New York City, let alone Europe.

Two months before my encounter in New York, I was caught speaking the Finnish language.

Finn was widely spoken in Astoria. My parents were primarily of Finnish descent. Both spoke Finn. Dad's parents, my Grandma and Grandpa, who lived a few blocks from us, spoke Finn almost exclusively. The new generation of our family—my sister, my brother, and me—had not caught on to the language, save for basic greetings and swear words. That is, until recently.

Our parents often spoke in Finn at the dinner table. They used it during arguments when they didn't want us kids to know what they were arguing about. This frustrated me but, ultimately, I was inspired. I vowed to learn Finn, without my parents' knowledge. I would crack their code.

At the public library, I dug up some primers that had been used by Finnish children during the early twentieth century. At Grandpa and Grandma's house, I found several books written in Finnish. I started to figure it out. As I developed a modest proficiency, I experimented with my new skills by speaking with

Grandpa and Grandma. They were ever so happy to help me learn.

I should have been more careful about what I asked for. As I began to understand the secrets my parents concealed, I sometimes wished I had, as Jane sometimes said, left well enough alone.

Eventually, I was exposed.

I sat with Grandma and Grandpa on their sunporch, chatting—in Finn. Dad clambered up the stairs to the porch and sat down with us. The conversation continued. I was so comfortable with Finn that I forgot it was the language of the moment. However, Dad noticed.

"Pekka!" he exclaimed, calling me by my Finnish name. He gazed at the sky. His eyes flitted back and forth as if recalling secrets that were no more, that probably hadn't been secret for a while. "Kauhea," he said in Finn: This is dreadful.

That weekend Aunt Helen and Uncle Bill came to visit. They observed my communication with my grandparents. Their reaction was joyful. Within a few days, it was worked out: I was going to Scandinavia with Helen and Bill. For the summer!

But first came New York City. We rolled through some museums. We met up with Jack's college roommate, Richard, who lived in the City. We zoomed up the Empire State Building. We experienced a Broadway play ("Half a Sixpence"). We went to fancy stores and stayed in a wonderful hotel on 49th Street. I even had my own room.

The night before we were to board the plane in which we would cross the Atlantic, Helen and Bill seemed pretty exhausted. At about ten that night they said goodnight to me at the door to my room. I went inside—for a few minutes.

I couldn't resist experiencing just a little more of New York City, although I wasn't sure of what that meant. I hopped into an elevator, trying to get to street level. It stopped before it got there. I got off the elevator and noticed another one down the hall. The new elevator was adorned with brass and mahogany. It had a stool for the attendant, who was nowhere to be seen. I entered. There was a button with a down arrow...

The elevator opened to a small room with a very high ceiling. It was a classy back-stage area. A bartender stood behind an ornate bar. Another gentleman sat on a bench by a baby grand piano.

I was ready to apologize and get the heck out of there. The man at the piano rose gently and asked how I was able to commandeer the elevator. I mumbled something about a logical button. He laughed and asked me about my accent.

"West Coast?"

"Oregon."

He nodded. "What's your story, son?"

I recognized him, but couldn't pull out the name.

Nervously, I started to explain about secretly learning Finn, getting caught and all.

"Peter, come on over and sit with me. My name is Duke Ellington." He gestured to the bartender. "Bring this fellow a Coke."

We talked for a bit. Mr. Ellington was fascinating, and he seemed genuinely curious about my short life. He moved with great elegance.

As I got back into the elevator, Mr. Ellington waved and gave me a big smile.

"Peter," he said. "Helsinki is a beautiful town. Enjoy it with your aunt and uncle.

WAKE UP AND SMELL THE COFFEE

When I wake up, sometimes the first thing I notice is sound—perhaps music, talking, or a car horn. Other times, my eyes take the lead. Then the first thing I notice is an image or a light. This day it was a smell. I had fallen asleep with my face was buried in a bag of coffee which was ground just two days before in a pastry shop in Denmark. The smell was wonderful; I woke up savoring it.

"Come on. Time to rise. We're at the burial ship." Uncle Bill sounded more excited than impatient.

Aunt Helen was bustling, too.

Burial ship? I got out of the Volkswagen van, where I'd dozed off, and looked around. I didn't see a ship. Uncle Bill was closing up the van. I grabbed my camera.

A short path took us to a hill with a metal door in it. That was odd. Aunt Helen pulled the door open while Uncle Bill took her picture. She didn't look at the camera because Uncle Bill likes people to be candid, to pretend that they don't know he has a camera.

Once we got past the door, we were in an entryway. The walls, floor, and ceiling were metal. The space narrowed to a metal tunnel that sloped down for about fifty feet. Metal pipes on the ceiling ran between dim lights. A sign said, among other things in Swedish, German, and English, that we weren't allowed to take photographs using a flash. Bill grumbled about that. He had a flash-attachment in his bag.

When we got to the bottom of the tunnel, we entered a big cave and saw a boat about sixty-feet long with both ends tapered. At its widest place, it was about twelve feet. This was a fairly simple boat, somewhat like a large canoe, except that the bow and stern rose higher than on canoes I had seen, even the concrete version of Chief Comcomly's burial canoe near the Astoria Column.

Was this a burial ship? Should I even be here?

Aunt Helen must have read my expression. She said, "This ship predates the Vikings. Someone special was buried in it, but they don't know who."

"What about this cave?" I said. "It looks modern."

"It is," said Helen. "All this was buried. The archeologists have carefully removed the dirt. They want to keep the ship down here to study."

"What about the--uh..."

"They've removed the skeleton."

That was my question, not that the answer made me feel any better. What came to my mind was a very scary mummy story that Jane had frightened me with. Was I hanging out with grave robbers? Was the ceiling of the cave about to collapse?

"Come over here," said Uncle Bill. "This is an interesting angle, even if we can't use a flash."

I didn't feel so well, but I preferred photography class to learning more about what they're doing with the skeleton.

When we got out of that cave, the Swedish air was delicious.

I sat in the back of the van. In about an hour, Bill pulled over. For hitchhikers!

Wow, this was a surprise. My mother and Dad never stopped for hitchhikers. Dad called them hobos, and my mother said they were dangerous. Jane was the only person in my family who picked up hitchhikers. I hitched rides when I wanted to go to Coffenbury Lake or the beach or even across town, but I never told my parents.

We made room in the back for a woman and a man, their bags and guitars. It turns out we had picked up Gunnel & Jan, the folk singers. They were touring Sweden, performing, and selling their 45 rpm record. Their destination was only eighty miles away. Gunnel spoke English well. She said the weather was beautiful. She said they would rather hitch a ride and meet new people than take a smelly bus.

Gunnel gave us a free record. Gunnel & Jan's destination turned out to be a nice hotel and restaurant. We decided to stay there for the night. Our new friends played during dinner and afterward. They were great. Besides songs in Swedish, they played "Homeward Bound," "Nowhere Man," "If I Were a Carpenter," "Puff, the Magic Dragon," and "Blowin' in the Wind," and more! I stayed up late.

☯

A few weeks later, we were in a little town in Finland. The town had two churches. There was a big wooden one that reminded me of Auntie Irma's Lutheran church in Astoria. The other church was made from stone that looked so old it might have been dropped off by a glacier.

We had visited lots of churches. Aunt Helen loved to go to churches to learn about our relatives and other people's relatives. The churches kept records about baptisms, weddings, and funerals. She wanted to go to the big new church first. I felt drawn to the stone church.

"They won't let you take pictures at all in there," said Uncle Bill.

"That's all right," I said.

☯

Bill went with Helen. I was on my own with the stone church. There was a sign out front that indicated photography was prohibited. There was also a story on the sign, but it was hard to read, something about a pastor named Nicolaus Rungius who died in 1629. Before he died, he said that if his words were true, his body wouldn't decay. That was weird.

I followed a path around the church to an open door. Stone

stairs descended into the church. Each step down the air got colder, until it was almost freezing, even though it was probably sixty-degrees outside.

At the bottom of the stairs, I walked into a relatively large, cross-shaped room. The stone ceiling was terrific. The rocks fit together perfectly, even though this place was like 400 years old. No one else was there.

My eyes shifted down to a horizontal display case about six feet long and thirty inches wide. It had a glass top. I walked over to check it out.

There laid the mummy of Nicolaus Rungius. I didn't need a photograph; I talked myself into memorizing every excruciating detail.

Jane would hear about this.

EMMA AND THE WITCH

Grandma had exceptional upper body strength. It stayed with her as an octogenarian. She was spry as an arctic fox.

Her friends called her Emma. Grandma guarded the traditions of her ancestors. She was born in the 1880s in Risudden, Sweden, across the Tornio River from Finland, a toss of a sauna rock from the arctic circle.

She insisted on drinking fresh raw milk, preferably delivered daily by the dairies. Every morning she'd set out glasses of raw milk so it would warm to room temperature by the time she and Grandpa sat down at noon for their big meal of the day. If houseflies were in season, she'd slip a square of waxed paper over the glasses.

Grandma baked cardamum bread for regular consumption and sliced some to use for korpu—a buttery, sugary, cinnamon zwieback favored by Grandpa, and almost everyone, for dipping in coffee.

Once a week, Grandma baked ten loaves of bread, following her own delicious recipe for limpu—a sponge-based whole wheat bread with rye, molasses, orange peel, and proprietary trace ingredients. She had a large metal bowl that she would rub down with butter when it was time to knead the dough—all ten loaves at once. With determination, with joy masquerading as pride, Grandma threw a towel under the bowl to protect the linoleum. Down on her knees, sleeves up, she powerfully worked the dough. Each week, Grandma shared the bread with family and good friends.

The kitchen where she baked was larger than the living

room, even larger than the dining room with the long table. It was the largest room in the house.

In the kitchen, there was a refrigerator and a free-standing stove. The sink and cupboards were in the adjacent pantry. When Grandpa built the house, in 1908, the original stove burned wood, as the decorative flue-plate on the chimney attested.

Most perishables were originally kept in cupboards with screens that allowed the flow of outside air. In those days, Dad taught me, the cooling cupboards were supplemented by a furniture-quality icebox.

The house was built with an upstairs bathroom, complete with a tub. Extra rooms anticipated children. I imagined the discussions about the plans for that house. I expected it was with pleasure that Grandpa listened to the wishes of his bride.

One feature of their house I could never figure out: The basement was constructed with beams barely five feet from the floor. A similar obstruction was encountered going down the basement stairway from the kitchen. Inevitably, each of the grandchildren would grow sufficiently to bonk their heads. I tried to get an explanation from Grandpa a couple of times, but he'd always scoff—and spit tobacco juice.

When I visited Grandpa's childhood home, built in the 1830s up the river from Ii (pronounced "ē"), in northern Finland, I felt instantly at home. The great room was dimensionally similar to Grandma and Grandpa's kitchen, as was the adjoining pantry.

The relatives who lived in that house still preferred a wood cookstove with warming racks. The entry to their pantry featured a five-foot dowel installed about a foot below the ceiling. The dowel accommodated over a dozen flat rounds of rye-tack. A new round would be added every couple days to one end of the dowel, as another fully crisp one was removed from the other end. Savory.

The sauna building was a stroll away, or a scamper in the winter. The sweating room was about six feet by fifteen feet—

long and hot. I was informed that Grandpa had been born in the dressing room.

☯

Occasionally, Grandma served as a consultant for people building a house or placing furniture. There was a folk tradition in the land of her birth to place furniture, especially beds, in harmony with the magnetic flows of the earth. Near the North Pole, mapped directions and magnetic directions increasingly diverge, so there was work for consultants. This divergence is not so great in northern Oregon, but it exists.

Grandma swung a gold watch on a chain to help determine fine adjustments to the layout of foundations and to help her envision recommendations for the interior design of homes.

Grandma used her pendulum setup other times. Sometimes an acquaintance of hers would stop by without the usual fanfare of a family get-together. Grandma and the visitors spoke Finn or Swedish or some combination thereof. Often that watch and chain came out, and Grandma swung it. Sometimes I saw money—most often a twenty-dollar bill—pass to Grandma's hand.

I got some clue as to what might be going on when I visited a witch in Finland. Aunt Helen and Uncle Bill learned about a woman who may have taught mystic arts to Grandma.

"Let's go see her," was my immediate response. They agreed.

One challenge was that this witch-teacher lived up the river in an isolated spot that could only be reached by a low-draft boat.

Bless Helen and Bill. They found a man with a small boat who was willing to take us to see the mysterious woman. He knew of her and where she lived but explained that he would only go see her if he had a hopeless terminal illness.

Let's go! I couldn't wait.

It seemed like an hour before we reached the witch-teacher's dock. Our boatswain wouldn't even step out of his vessel, so I tied up the boat.

As I finished securing the craft, a very wrinkled woman appeared on the dock. It was her!

She introduced herself and then promptly explained to Helen and Bill that they must stay on the dock. The young man —me—was welcome to come to her home. Maybe she had a one-person-per-day visitor rule? Whatever. I'll go!

And I did.

She led me a short way on a deteriorating plank path through the wetlands to her house—a cottage at that. I indulged a quick recollection from a couple of weeks prior, when we visited Hans Christian Andersen's house, in Denmark...

"I am not afraid," I said to myself. "I am curious."

In the house, numerous bundles of plants hung to dry. A mixture of unidentified odors hit my olfactory region, but I didn't sneeze.

She motioned for me to sit at a table. I gave her the pile of Finnish money that Helen had handed me as we left the dock. The woman took it and laughed. She poured tea for us.

It turned out she spoke some English. She knew we were staying in the area. Most importantly, she remembered Grandma.

I didn't know what to ask, so I sipped the tea. Oh my gosh, it was foul!

She caught the look on my face and laughed again. I enjoyed her laugh.

"Try again," she said and motioned to my cup.

I didn't want to, but I remembered Aunt Helen's travel advice: "When in Rome, be polite; you might learn something."

I sipped. I didn't freak out. It was good.

She smiled and told me about Grandma—as a teenager!

She told me they both danced around the midsummer bonfires by the river. They were about the same age.

The teacher had learned healing, geomancy (as near as I could understand), and native plants (I got that). I wanted to know what she meant by healing, but the language differences were too much of a barrier.

"Your grandmother had intuition," she said in near-perfect English.

She showed me several plants and told me that they could affect people's health by modifying their mood. Again, my understanding was limited by a lack of words we both could understand.

I voluntarily took another sip of the now-delicious tea.

I liked her. She was older than Grandma, but she seemed much younger. I felt gratitude. I hoped she could see it in my face.

It was time to go. We walked the path through the wetlands back to the dock.

She hid her face and snarled when Uncle Bill raised his fine Leica M3 camera. She walked away.

Aunt Helen and Uncle Bill boarded the boat. I untied the mooring lines.

I was glad that the noise from the outboard motor rendered talking unrealistic.

I just wanted to ponder what my new friend meant by intuition.

UNCLE PETER

The butter churn seemed like an antique to me, as did some other objects in the old shop building. There were several wooden canteens. There were chairs with hinged seats.

The canteens were carved from solid birch. Some came with a pouch made from reindeer hide with fur still intact. Uncle Peter crafted these with hand tools and decorated them with symbols unfamiliar to me. He sold many of these canteens every year to field workers—to use for their buttermilk.

Most of my immediate family enjoyed buttermilk. I detested it, but I said nothing in that regard. I even turned my head so my paternal great uncle would be spared my scowl of disgust.

I was thirteen, on my first trip to Lapland, and I'd just met Uncle Peter that morning. I was fascinated by my namesake and certainly did not want to offend him.

I redirected the conversation to the chairs.

"We pull up this," He explained, as he lifted the seat to reveal a boxed-in area. To me, it seemed like a flat toilet seat. He picked up some old leather boots, stuffed them with straw, and put them in the box. He threw in some more straw, then closed the lid. He stood up and smiled, like a student demonstrating his project.

I got it. You stuff your boots at the end of the day so they'll retain their shape as they dry out by morning. He built these chairs and decorated them with rosemaling designs from the nineteenth century.

Now it was time for the butter churn. It was not an antique, at least not the way that Uncle Peter figured. He had built it when he was about my age, so I calculated its inception as being about the year 1906. He had replaced parts a few times over the decades.

The churn was fully functional. In the blink of a twinkling eye, Uncle Peter poured cream into the machine as I turned the crank. After far too long for my attention span, the thing turned cream into butter.

Uncle Peter smiled and mimed a cranking motion. "Keep up."

Eventually, he deemed the butter satisfactory. I shook my wrist and thanked my uncle.

We walked over to the main house. Wow. Nearly the entire house was dedicated to the repair and decorative painting of wooden grandfather and wall clocks. He fixed cracks and broken details. He made adjustments to the mechanisms of time-keeping. He reproduced painting from multiple eras of Swedish and Finnish design.

I was drawn to a group of clocks of minimalist woodworking, painted with strikingly unusual yet somehow familiar symbols. This was a project of which Uncle Peter seemed particularly proud. It was a restoration at the behest of a native Saami family.

We had dinner at the house with my American aunt and uncle, Helen and Bill, who had been sight-seeing for the afternoon.

Uncle Peter headed to bed pretty early by my inclination, turning off his old-school hearing aid as he walked from the room. I was in the habit of watching the late-June sun descend to touch the horizon, only to then begin its ascent. This being the farthest north I had ever been, I wanted to stay up for the midnight phenomena. But I was tired, so I went to my tiny room and immediately dozed off.

"Clang. Clang. Clang. Clang..."

I was startled awake by one of those many clocks. Okay, back to sleep.

"Bong. Bong. Bong..."

Hey! That wasn't an hour.

"Tang. Tang. Tang. Tang. Tang. Tang…"

That wasn't fifteen minutes.

Then I put it together: Uncle Peter lives alone in this house. He repairs clocks. He uses hearing aids. The clocks are all set for different times. I wasn't going to get much sleep.

I somehow tuned-out the chimes for a couple of hours, but eventually, I gave up and wandered into the morning light. I walked through a large field. I traced the edge of a forest that transitioned from dominant birch with maple and alder, near as I could tell, to a mix of pines.

Then I came upon her.

What the heck was she? She was larger than a deer, smaller than an elk, nothing like a moose, with no horns.

She didn't seem startled. I didn't bother her at all. Still, she was pretty big.

I looked toward Uncle Peter's house. It wasn't in sight, but I figured it was two, maybe closer to three miles distant.

I gave the mammal a little bow. I have no idea why. Then I turned and ran all the way to the house.

I caught my breath as I opened the back door and entered the kitchen. Uncle Peter was having coffee. He wanted to know what was up with me.

In awkward Finnish, I explained how I was out for a walk when I came upon a most unusual creature.

Uncle Peter said, "Poro."

It wasn't a burro. I knew that for sure. Neither donkey nor ass, not even a mule. And it wasn't an antelope. I was starting to think maybe it was a weird type of elk.

"Poro," Uncle Peter insisted. He laughed.

I was at the edge of an argument with a very special relative.

Then Uncle Bill showed up. He was haggard. I could see he hadn't slept, and I knew why.

I explained the mammal controversy.

"Poro is Finnish for reindeer," he muttered as he reached

for a coffee cup.

Oh.

"Ding dong. Ding dong. Ding dong..."

SURTSEY

During the plane voyage from New York to Helsinki, I was wide-eyed as we flew into the dawn.

We landed to refuel at Reykjavik. After takeoff, the pilot generously improvised a fly-over of Surtsey, an island in formation in the ocean south of Iceland.

On the return trip, I hoped to get another look at Surtsey. It was night, and I believe that all the passengers on the plane were asleep—except for me. As I peered out the window, I was dismayed to observe the right engine on fire. I thought perhaps I should tell someone, but even the flight attendants were snoozing in their chairs.

"Maybe it's better if they don't know," I thought.

I looked at the engine again. It was most certainly not normal. And the plane was descending.

Then the pilot's voice came over the cabin speakers. Shortly, we would be landing in Reykjavik.

The landing was okay. However, the pilot came on again and suggested that we quickly deplane. I didn't argue.

We spent about eight hours in the terminal, waiting until they could bring us another plane.

This time I volunteered for an aisle seat.

CHAPTER FIVE

HOME

HOMECOMING

CHEMISTRY

HEMLOCK

WHITTLING

HOMECOMING

Our house in Beaverton was a lot like the other houses on our street and the nearby streets. I walked around and studied them. I had one day to get to know my new neighborhood before my first day at school.

Some of the houses looked like the other ones would in a mirror. I thought of them as right-handed and left-handed, depending on which side the double garage doors were on.

Auntie Irma was left-handed, which meant that she could do a lot of things better with her left hand than her right hand, like sew and throw and cast. I knew some left-handed kids who held their pencil in their left hand when they wrote. Auntie Irma wrote with her right hand because her teacher made her do it, even though it was more difficult for her. That made me mad. She shouldn't have been punished for how she was born.

Walking and thinking like this, I noticed that I felt sad. I hadn't seen Auntie Irma since June when I went to Finland and some other countries. Now it was September. I missed her.

In June, my parents turned me over to Auntie Helen and Uncle Bill, who took me to Europe.

When I returned to the United States, I expected to go home to Astoria. That didn't happen. Now I lived almost one hundred miles away from the only town I'd known as home.

After we flew across Canada and then rented a car in Vancouver, British Columbia, Aunt Helen and Uncle Bill told me that my parents and I now lived in Beaverton. I don't know how they knew this or when they found out. I didn't ask them right away. I fell asleep...

They brought me to this strange neighborhood with right-handed and left-handed houses. We went to the door of one of them. Dad appeared. It was as if I was still on vacation, discovering new things every day.

Dad showed me my room. I didn't come out until morning.

The morning was weird.

I could tell Dad wanted to explain some things, but couldn't quite get started. He stood like he was a little off-balance. My mother was silent and strange. Neither of them touched me. Mother seemed afraid to touch me, which was fine, and Dad wasn't sure how to do it.

They were both uncomfortable. I wanted to fix that. I could take-on their uncomfortable feelings and put them in my belly. Then things would be more normal.

But I didn't do it. I had changed during the summer. I wasn't husky anymore. I was tall and slim. I had learned a way to pause before I fixed other people's feelings. No one had expected me to do the taking-on all summer. Now instead of automatically doing it, I could choose.

I suppose this technique has limits. I'll ask Jack as soon as I can.

"Hey, where is Jack?"

"He's in Portland, at school," said Dad.

"When will I see him?"

"Sometime soon."

Here I am in a strange place. Nobody bothered to tell me about it in advance. What about my friends?

If either of my parents feels sorry for not telling me, why don't they say so?

"I need to get my film developed," I said. "It won't cost much. I can cut the film in pieces and put the pictures in slide mounts myself. Then I can show you where I've been and what I did."

My mother's face didn't change.

"That's nice," she said. There was an extraordinary sadness. Avoiding taking-on was difficult.

I tried Dad.

"Where's your shop, Dad?"

"I don't need one," he said, flatly. "I'm a salesman now. I work for National Builders Hardware."

Auntie Helen and Uncle Bill's company. That was information. They did know about this. How long did they know? All summer? Longer? I was probably the only person who didn't know I was moving. A salesman? Like the Fuller Brush Man?

"How is Jane?"

Dad looked down, then at my mother.

"Jane is having a hard time."

I should be in Astoria helping my sister. I felt anger. I have zero control. I don't have any say about where I live or when I can see Jane.

"Where's my darkroom stuff?" Dad and I had built a darkroom in the basement at the house I'll never see again. Cousin Jimmy gave me enlargers and trays and other cool stuff. I loved that darkroom.

"In the family room. In those boxes over there."

Dad had helped me with lot's of stuff in the past few years. He helped with my science projects. One was called "Computer?" I explained the binary system and demonstrated how a simple machine could solve problems using punched note cards, wires, batteries, and flashlight bulbs. It was simple, almost silly, but I was so happy Dad helped me with it. I believed he was truly interested. I got a first-place trophy from the Oregon Museum of Science and Industry. Another project I entered was called "Pineal Body." My display was mostly words and pictures, with a long bibliography. Dad helped me build the display. He also suggested that I talk with Morris, a family friend. Some people called Morris a hermit, but he was a philosopher. I interviewed him about Descartes. That interview probably caused my project to win both an award as well as a scholarship for me to spend a week at science summer camp by Cape Blanco.

I knew inside this wasn't Dad's fault.

"I'm going to make waffles," said my mother.

Fine. Don't expect me to be interested in when the light on that thing goes out.

☯

I wish I had Superman hearing.

In May, before I left for Europe, two policemen in two cars

came to our Floral Street house in Astoria. I bolted down the stairs from my room, but Dad sent me back up.

"Come down after they leave," Dad said softly. He was very sad. And he was scared.

From the entryway of the house, you could turn left into the living room. Straight ahead in the entry was a door that opened to a steep stairway that went up to two bedrooms, for Jack and me, except Jack was at college.

Upstairs, I took off my shoes and sat down. I scooted down the stairs, almost to the bottom. I would look pretty silly if someone opened the door. But they didn't.

I could hear Dad inviting the police in. When they went into the living room, I couldn't hear as well, but I made out a few words: icepick...tires...accused...arrest...alcohol.

What was happening?

Mother started laughing. Dad told her to be quiet, in Finnish, loudly. That was different.

I could hear just enough that I felt worried but not enough to understand why: Grand jury...protect a child...jail.

When the police left, I opened the door and went into the living room. I guess my mother was in their bedroom. Dad looked like...I don't know what Dad looked like. I had heard people talk about a deer freezing in place when they look in headlights. I'd say that's what he looked like, but it was more than his eyes that were frozen.

Some houses, including ours, had a family room where the garage would be. A few had a big room above the garage or family room. The houses were painted with different colors.

When I got home from walking around the block, I ran out to the backyard. I climbed on the back fence. Just as I suspected, the back fences were the same all the way down the block.

I sat on the grass.

Tomorrow I would start eighth grade at a new school, in a new town. I felt fear. I also sensed that something interesting, something good would happen.

CHEMISTRY

Larry's favorite group was Simon and Garfunkel. I liked them, too, and I was fascinated by Bob Dylan. Of course, we were both fans of The Beatles and The Rolling Stones. He and I also listened to The Beach Boys.

I wasn't going to push it further. I'd keep Mose Allison and Pete Seeger in reserve.

Larry was the first kid I met in Beaverton. He lived around the corner. He wanted to know where I came from.

I decided to trust Larry. I told him about how my parents had summarily moved me with them from our home in Astoria while I was on a summer trip to northern Europe with my aunt and uncle. I was in the eighth grade in a strange school in a strange neighborhood.

Now at least I had one potential friend. Larry did all he could to be kind and friendly. He had a record player in the garage at his house where we listened to music.

It was a sunny September Saturday. Larry's mom brought us apples and shooed us outside. Why not!

The neighborhood houses were all similar. I commented on that. In Astoria, almost every house was different.

"I've got something to show you," Larry said. He led me down the street to a place where the road made a ninety-degree turn. There was a patch of trees and an almost-hidden trail. A few steps in and I felt at home. The alder forest reminded me of the Little Woods in the town where I had spent my entire life, until now.

I expected the trail would take us to more suburban tract houses, but it didn't. We came out of the woods to a farm—with a barn. There was a kid about our age in the barn, working at a grinding wheel.

"Hey Chris," shouted Larry. "Come meet Peter."

Chris switched off the grinder.

"What?" Chris pulled on his ear.

"This is Peter."

Chris stuck out his hand like a grownup and shook mine. He was lanky. His hands and his overalls were dirty. Excellent. I've met another potential friend.

"I can't play now. Dad expects me to have all of these chisels sharpened by three."

"That's okay. I'm just showing Peter around."

"Good to meet you, Peter. Come 'round anytime."

We walked back into the woods.

"Chris has to work with his dad a lot. Sometimes he has to miss school."

☯

There was a small hill at the edge of the forest. It reminded me of the clay hill behind the house that Dad built on Pleasant Avenue. It was the second house he built on that street, but I couldn't remember living in the first one.

A few years back, I was at the clay hill out behind our house. I planned to test my grenade.

Cousin Jimmy gave my brother Jack his old chemistry set. I think Jack got bored with it, so it became mine. When I took all the chemicals and equipment out of the storage box, I saw there was an extra piece of cardboard the same size as the bottom of the box. I used my pocket knife to pry the cardboard out.

Underneath were several sheets of paper with hand-written notes. Cool.

I read the notes. They were recipes for making chemical reactions. These projects were much more interesting than the ideas that came with the set. There was a mixture that made a liquid that could be dried on a hard surface. Once dry, you could throw rocks at it, and it would make a popping sound. That seemed useful. There was a recipe for gunpowder. I might be careful with that. There were notes on how to make a grenade, although a bunch of the writing was smeared. There was a discussion about different types of rocket fuel. This was a jackpot!

I memorized some of the ingredients and went to the library. I found instructions to make gunpowder in a book. It looked the same as on the note. I couldn't find any of the other recipes. I would have to experiment.

The grenade sounded interesting. There were five jars of chemicals that Jimmy included with the set that were too large to fit in the box. A few were needed for gunpowder, and a couple more were needed to make grenades. I had a beaker where I mixed up my best guess of the grenade ingredients, except I didn't use any shrapnel. Did Jimmy do this a lot? Is that why he had the big jars?

The problem was I didn't have a detonator. I wondered if I could use gunpowder to set it off. One way to find out.

I took the beaker packed with chemicals out to the clay hill and found a level spot. I dug a little hole for my beaker and packed clay soil around it. I had sliced a channel in a rubber stopper that fit the beaker. I poured out a bunch of the gunpowder that I'd mixed up, filling the channel and making a trail of gunpowder that went across the clay a few feet.

I surveyed the area. There was no one around. I didn't expect this to work anyway.

I had borrowed a little box of matches from the downstairs fireplace. I struck one and touched the flame to the gunpowder. The match went out. I tried it again. This time the gunpowder started burning. I ran toward our house, then I laid down on the lawn and covered my head like on *Death Valley Days*, still not expecting anything to happen. It did.

There was an explosion. Dirt flew. I was terrified. What had I done?

I waited, wondering if there would be another explosion. I thought the police would come any minute. Surely, someone would ask them to investigate.

I had to look. Even from several yards away I could see that there was a hole in the ground two feet across and nearly that deep. I decided it would be best if I turned myself in to ask the judge for mercy.

I went into the house to tell my mother. She was watching the television. I confessed what I had done.

"That's nice."

"What do you mean, nice? I made an explosion."

"I didn't hear anything. You should send Cousin Jim a thank-you card."

There was a hose in the backyard that had a metal piece on the end where the water could be turned on and adjusted to spray or shoot out. I adjusted it so it would send the water the farthest. I aimed at my explosion hole and soaked the area.

I put the hose back and headed down the trail to Bob's store. Maybe I would get away with this.

☯

"Hey, Peter. Do you want to shoot some hoops?" Larry had a basketball hoop outside his garage.

"Sounds good to me."

HEMLOCK

There was a tall western hemlock tree next to my Beaverton room. It had somehow escaped the placement of houses. It pretty much blocked access through the side yard to the back.

On the side of my bedroom where the tree was, there were no windows. If you didn't look up and over while you were outside the house, you might not know the tree was there. I lived in that house for three days before I noticed the tree.

Once I knew it existed, I felt the tree. I had a relationship with a hemlock. Its presence on the other side of the wall was a non-visible inspiration for my meditation practice. It just stood there, tall and humble.

My sister Jane taught me to notice my thoughts and feelings, and to take a breath if I couldn't seem to catch up. I think she prescribed this to help me with my difficulties.

"Notice, don't control," she explained. "Let go of Evil. Fast."

This helped me stop my mother from adding more secrets. I developed a warning system that I named: "I don't know what to call it, but it's wrong." I could go straight from meditation to fighting.

By the time I was thirteen I was always ready to fight to protect my body from my mother. The attitude itself kept her away. It helped that I was stronger than I'd ever been.

When I was in Finland, Aunt Helen said it was fine to sit on the ground, or the floor, or on a chair and do nothing.

I thought her dad, my Grandpa, did something like this when he let out his breath, smiling like there was nothing left to do, letting the syllables hang as he sighed, "No, yo."

I asked Aunt Helen about this. She slapped her knee like Walter Brennan in *The Real McCoys* when she laughed.

I'm glad I learned the ready-to-fight stuff before I read Gandhi's life story and considered ahimsa—nonviolence toward all. At the time, anger that threatened to escalate into violence was a valued if specialized emotion. It dawned on me in Finland, where I felt completely safe, that intentionally not using a powerful emotion to stop a bad thing from happening could itself be violence. But who decides what is bad? Yeah, I was still confused, but I felt better.

Back in the United States, I asked my brother Jack about meditation. He gave me a copy of the *Bhagavad Gita.* I didn't get it. Two brothers on opposing sides in a civil war try to kill each other, and that's okay because all of our lives are tangled up like an overused gill net, and everyone wants to get free and dance into an atom. I returned the book.

Jack touched the whiskers on his chin when I told him I probably understood it all wrong but does he have something else? I wanted to explain to him what I needed meditation for but the words stuck in my throat.

"This isn't for you," he said as he wagged his finger and smiled at the wall. He handed the book back to me. "Not yet."

The next week, Jack brought me *The Three Pillars of Zen.* I loved it. I practiced zazen in addition to the Watching I learned from Jane. Together they were my remedy for some of the icky nervous things in my belly.

I softened toward myself. I didn't need to always be on the edge of violence to be safe. Rather than constantly stay defensive, I could follow my interests. Who else would follow them?

I felt a warm, outgoing sensation; a big thank you. My sister and my brother had combined their good intentions in an attempt to save my life. I wanted to live to be an adult if only to reward my sister and brother for their caring.

There was a partial release in my chest. This felt like a dirty trick because I was aware of the possibility of a full release —a satisfying breath—but I couldn't experience it. Yet, I noticed if I sincerely appreciated the partial release, gratitude itself gifted me a useful, if not fully satisfying, energy.

Energy that I didn't use always being ready to fight for myself could be used to help others; Dad, for instance. I could tell that he felt defeated putting on a coat and tie and trying to be a salesman. He gave up his life. For what? Finances? Whatever it was that those policemen talked about with Dad and my mother? It didn't matter. I could feel his pain. I could give him love without losing my own, albeit still-limited, energy.

Instead of remaining righteously indignant about getting displaced from Astoria, I enjoyed my new home and school and being close to Portland. I began ninth grade in a new program based around ideologies. I had followed math as far as I wanted, for now.

There was a war in Vietnam. I'd been reading and thinking and talking about it since sixth grade. Now I felt about it. I wanted to end it. What could I do? I didn't think that getting tear gas on my face was a good choice for me.

Senator Eugene McCarthy, a poet, was running for president. I could help him win. He'll end the war.

I called the McCarthy for President office in Portland and told them that I wanted to help Senator McCarthy win. Two people got on the line and asked if I would volunteer. Yes. They asked if I liked to make phone calls. Sure. They asked me what county I lived in. Washington. They asked me if I knew any Republicans. Two were right here in my household.

"Come on down. Let's talk. We need someone to work with our Republicans for McCarthy program in Washington County."

I hitchhiked to Portland.

When the two campaign leaders saw me, they were disappointed. I couldn't even vote, they moaned.

I told them I knew that, and I knew that a Republican couldn't vote for Senator McCarthy in the Democratic primary unless they registered as a Democrat. I told them that I'd met Senator Hatfield, a Republican, and I know he wants peace. And I know he's popular. I told them I was certain that many Republicans wanted the war to end and they'd change their registration to make a difference—if one of their neighbors asked them to, like me. I'll mostly be talking on the phone. They won't know how old I am, just how motivated. My voice has changed.

"On the phone, you thought that you were talking with an adult. Didn't you?"

They welcomed me to the campaign team. I persuaded dozens of Washington County Republicans to register as Democrats. Many of these Republicans, my parents included, permitted me to use their names in campaign ads endorsing Senator McCarthy. Quite a few met me and had no problem with my age.

Senator McCarthy won the Oregon primary. I stood near him, celebrating as the results came in. I thought about telling him that I was a poet, too, but I didn't want to dilute the moment.

☯

It was time to move again. This time, we returned to the Astoria area. Our home was about six miles out of town, near Greenwood Cemetery.

This was a pretty isolated spot, but I would have moved to the moon to see Dad happy again.

That winter, I learned that the western hemlock next to my Beaverton bedroom fell in a windstorm. My unoccupied room was crushed.

WHITTLING

I wasn't very good at whittling, but I took to carrying a pocketknife. I enjoyed sharpening the blade on Dad's special stone.

In the summer preceding my Sophomore year in high school, my parents moved us to a rented house in the country, by Youngs River. It was a unique location: A state highway caressed the front yard. Across the highway, tidal forces of the Columbia River estuary revealed the muddy shallows of Youngs River twice a day. A graveyard was mere steps away from our house.

Dad made his escape from Beaverton just as I was becoming enamored of life around Portland. I could sense how bad he felt about trying to be a salesman. He was a creator—a master woodworker, and a storyteller besides.

Dad created new kitchens and bathrooms for his customers. He was a pioneer in the installation of Formica.

Earlier in his life, he worked in the carpentry shop at Astoria Marine Construction Company. He called it AMCCO. It was a big company, with its own newspaper. At AMCCO, Dad created cabinetry out of woods such as teak and mahogany. He worked on yachts and fishing boats and government projects.

☯

Cars and trucks went fast on the highway by our house. When I had a chance, I'd run across the road, and climb down to the banks of the river. I adopted a nice private spot with a boulder I could sit on and a tree limb to rest my back against. I never saw anyone else there, so I considered it my special place.

At high tide, carp swam to the shoreline of my special place. I made some half-hearted efforts to catch them with dough balls on a hook, but it was too easy. They didn't fight for their lives like salmon, trout, and steelhead did. I didn't want to eat the carp, so I let them go. It just wasn't fun.

My special place was great for meditation. It was comfortable, and the noise of the cars was muffled.

Sometimes memories appeared during meditation. Once I remembered a scene from when I was six. It was at our house on Pleasant Avenue. I was alone with my mother. Her voice changed into a fierce cackle. She hit me in the face with an ashtray.

I tried to stop the decade-old memory. It was supposed to stay with the secrets.

"Go away," I said aloud, startling myself. It wouldn't. Instead, the memory continued.

I barely had time to be shocked by the blow to my face when my mother overpowered me and threw me on the sectional couch—the ugly scratchy maroon sectional couch.

She straddled my six-year-old body. She grabbed the quilt of knitted squares of wool, the quilt Grandma had made to celebrate my birth. She shoved the heavy fabric into the face of younger me.

Suddenly, the six-year-old me floated near the ceiling of the living room, witnessing his assault. Then my mother stopped. She removed the quilt. The six-year-old by the ceiling faded.

With a sweet voice, she said, "Oh, look. What has happened to your face? You've had an accident. Come with your mother. Let's put some ointment on that."

☯

When my consciousness returned to my special place by the river, my hand fingered my pocketknife.

In the days and weeks to come, I found that my special place was a good spot to drink fruit wines from the bottle —loganberry and apple. I discovered that uninvited memories would not visit, or at least would not stick around if I drank wine.

Whenever I had the chance to use my pocketknife, such as sharpening sticks to hold hot dogs over a fire, I demonstrated my improving whittling skills within the view of my mother.

CHAPTER SIX

TRIP

PROHIBITION

FALL BREAK

PERMANENT RECORD

LEAP YEAR

JAAKO

ROCK PILE

PROHIBITION

In 1968, Bob Packwood narrowly defeated Wayne Morse to win election as a US Senator from Oregon. I was disappointed.

I first met Senator Morse when I was twelve years old, at a rally in support of commercial fishermen. Two years later, I walked along Broadway in downtown Portland and almost passed by the Senator. He stopped me.

"Peter," said Senator Morse. He held up a finger. "A Finn name, something like Hootah. Am I right?"

"Huhtala," I replied.

"Yup. You were standing for the rights of fishermen. In Astoria?"

"Salem."

"I remember now. Peter, always speak your truth and champion your beliefs. Nobody sees things exactly like you. Speak up."

"Thank you for your stand against the Vietnam War, Senator."

"I appreciate that. When enough of us agree, we win."

He looked me straight in the eyes. He smiled as he shook my hand with a wise and robust grip.

☯

When Senator Packwood came to Astoria High School, I was on the staff of the student newspaper, the *Astor Post.* I was also on the debate team.

Packwood looked young, but he had a surly disposition

that day. I asked him about legalizing marijuana, and he practically scolded me for asking the question. He opposed legalization and considered marijuana to be a dangerous narcotic that leads to heroin addiction.

"You should study the subject," I replied. "Marijuana is far less harmful than alcohol, and there is no evidence that it is a gateway to hard drugs."

Senator Packwood retorted, "You're here to ask questions. I'll answer them."

"If you won't listen to the people, how can you represent us?"

"I represent the people who elected me, not a bunch of potheads!"

"Thoughtful answer, Senator. No further questions from me."

☯

I never smoked marijuana with Dad, or Jane, or Jack. My reasons were different for each of them. I figured Dad didn't need anything to add to his alcohol abuse. If he gave up the booze for marijuana, that would be great, but I couldn't see me arguing that case. Besides, I had never been honest with him about smoking pot. Maybe it was better to keep it as one of those things we don't talk about.

Jane didn't have an alcohol problem, but she had prescriptions. Sometimes she was a bit erratic. I wasn't sure if that was due to the prescriptions or somehow related to epilepsy—the disease that caused her to have seizures. Marijuana was a gentle herb, but some say it could cause paranoia. I suspected that people mistook paranoia for fear, such as the fear of getting caught with the illegal substance. It didn't matter. I wouldn't take a chance with anything that might even confuse my sister.

I could see offering Jack some weed. He went to Reed College. I wouldn't be surprised if he'd tried it. He married Bob's sister, Carolyn, though, and I didn't think Carolyn would smoke the stuff.

There was one time at a family get-together... Jack came upstairs to my room. Bob and I had just smoked some hash and burned incense to cover up the scent.

When Jack came in, he said, "Smells nice." I don't think he meant the incense. We'd smoked all the hash, so we didn't have anything to offer or hide.

Possibly, Jack was high already. The clue was his uproarious laugh when he listened to the intro to Jimi's "Voodoo Child - Slight Return."

Jack sputtered as he explained, "He told a joke with his guitar." Jack laughed some more. Yeah, he was probably high.

Several months prior, Jack, Bob, and I went on a camping and fishing trip. And such a trip it was. We camped at Fall River, near Bend, Oregon. We had a couple of fly rods and flies with barbless hooks. We traded off catching and releasing the abundant trout.

One day we each caught a toad, with our hands. Jack promoted toad-racing. Bob was a little shy about this at first, but he got into it. At least he was a good sport. We used sticks for the starting and finish lines, and for the out-of-bounds. We each had two chances to tickle our toads toward the finish line. The animals weren't particularly cooperative.

This sport reminded me of the garter snake races Jack and I had several years before. We tied two garden hoses together, side by side, with masking tape. Then we caught two snakes. We guided the snakes headfirst into the hoses and waited until they came out the other end. We let those snakes go. If we found more snakes, we did it again. One long red racer that Jack found was by far the fastest of all we drafted into the competition. I think the snakes warned the others about us because it was hard to find more garter snakes after a couple of races.

☯

On the last night of our journey, we camped near Mt. Hood,

at Harriet Lake. We cooked the steaks that Jack had bought in Madras. Jack drank a couple of beers and retired early to the big canvas tent. Bob and I had other plans.

Bob had acquired a tablet of Czechoslovakian Black Speck, a pharmaceutical grade of LSD from behind the Iron Curtain. We later learned that these tabs contained a consistent 1000 micrograms each of the, um, active ingredient. That was a lot. Owsley Stanley's products that contained 350-400 micrograms were generally considered four-way hits. Bob split the tablet in half, then down the hatches, they went.

This was my first LSD trip.

Bob and I were curious kids. I had shared with him what I had learned a few years before while researching my science project about the pineal gland. We were intrigued by the similar molecular structures of serotonin and psilocybin, a psychedelic present in magic mushrooms.

Bob was interested in my exploration of Zen Buddhism and Eastern philosophy in general. He spent a lot of time in libraries, exploring writings about consciousness-altering substances and practices. He acquired a treasured copy of Aldous Huxley's *Doors of Perception*.

Lysergic acid diethylamide was in the news and popular culture. A Harvard professor, Timothy Leary, suggested, "Turn on, tune in, drop out." Popular musicians did just that. The Beatles paisleyed-up their creative experiments with *Magical Mystery Tour*. The Jimi Hendrix Experience offered *Are You Experienced?* The Rolling Stones released *Their Satanic Majestic's Request*. The Doors presented their first album. What was it all about?

☯

"When the doors of perception are cleansed everything will appear as they really are, Infinite," quoted Bob.

"Nice fire," I said, as I put another piece of wood in place. "What now?"

"Wait. See."

"Have you done this before?"

"Once. I took a quarter tab."

We were both in new territory as we anticipated without expectation. We sat on a comfortable log and stayed warm by the fire.

"Hey, look. There's a bug on you," said Bob.

I looked at the back of my hand. There was a small colorful insect that grew wings and flew off. I looked at Bob's hand and said, "There's a bunch of bugs on you."

No sooner had I said it, but five unique styles of bugs were on Bob's hand. It seemed we could control this. We traded back and forth, elaborating on the bug theme.

A high-pitched sound grew louder in the dark sky. It was upon us in an instant—a mosquito about two feet in diameter bore down upon us, injector first. Simultaneously, we both felt backward off of the log.

"Do you think we should tell Jack about this?" I queried.

"Sure." Bob offered an example: "Jack, we were peacefully using our imaginations for bug games. Yeah, we were sharing hallucinations of ever more wild looking bugs, trying to scare each other. Uninvited, a giant mosquito came after us, and we fell off the log."

We looked at each other. Our upper torsos were in the dirt; our calves rested on a log. "Probably best to let him sleep," I said.

My eyes focused on a piece of bark still attached to the log, where tiny mammals engaged in a miniature trapeze circus routine. I could move if I wanted to, but this was entertaining.

Coals of the fire rubbed against each other in a complex unity. A warm snap released a spaceship from the interior of a spark. Hamsters in antique diving suits waved at athletes racing on the rings of Saturn. It went on like this for a while.

"Let's go walk," said Bob. He stood with his shoes near me and his head in Andromeda.

"Why not?" I had to think this through. I needed to rearrange my body, use my arms to push up, balance in harmony with gravity. Okay, let's walk. I pointed myself past Carolyn's red Volkswagen bug and onto the gravel road as silent images of my body echoed behind me. Yes, that's how it was: Echoes of vision. I stopped. Crunchy sounds approached from behind. I swiveled my head. There was Bob. He had body vision echoes, too. His face kept changing from lion to seal to penguin to caveman to Jiminy Cricket.

Harriet Lake was beside us. I could feel her sound, a rich metallic om.

"Try this." Bob waved an arm in front of his face. Dozens of arms and hundreds of fingers followed. I waved my arm, and something similar occurred. I spun an arm in a fast circle. It became a propeller. I flew over the top of Mt. Hood. Time disappeared. A molten caldera appeared, melting the rock and mud, sending a monstrous avalanche toward Hood River. The people in the path of the avalanche rode on a long escalator to a waiting ark suspended in the air.

I flew back to Harriet Lake and found Bob. His expression indicated he'd been up to similar adventures. We heard a car.

"Let's hide," I said. We crouched in the bushes.

Two race cars from 1910 pulled up in front of us. The drivers wore leather helmets. A woman in one of the cars waved a flag, and the cars took off, splattering gravel and leaving psychedelic dust in the air. It tasted like movie candy.

Jack awoke a little after the inspiring dawn. The three of us silently arranged a marvelous breakfast, then loaded the Volkswagen. As we reached a paved road, I turned the radio on. Blood, Sweat & Tears played "Spinning Wheel" through the crappy speaker. It was exquisite. Absolutely profound. Endless love expanded in all directions, inside and out.

FALL BREAK

It was late September in Astoria. Chinook and coho salmon were in the estuary chomping mackerel, sand lance, and herring. They were fattening up to complete the journey of their life.

After their years in the ocean, salmon enter the estuary to feed until they sensed the time was right to scoot up the Columbia River to the stream of their origin. Some swim hundreds of miles to reach the very same ripples and gravels where they'd hatched.

On a single-minded quest, the fish return home to spawn and die. This might have been tragic if it wasn't so cool.

Bob and I never tired of discussing the lives of salmon. We also loved to eat them—and catch them. Sometimes we camped near the South Jetty where we would catch the feeding fish with bait. In 1970, the road to the jetty was gravel and sand, but Bob's dad would get us out there, and return daily to pick up our catch.

Other times we would fish off the islands and beaches further up the river, using lures to catch the mighty fish.

This September it seemed that neither option was going to work out. Salmon were on the run. We were stuck in high school.

There had to be a way, but we couldn't see it.

☯

"I figured it out," Bob said, looking up from his guitar. "It starts on D."

Soon we were playing all the chords to "After the Gold Rush" by Neil Young. The album of the same name had just been released. We studied the lyrics and learned to play the songs.

I was writing a review of the album for our high school newspaper, the *Astor Post.* It was due in two days, as was my editorial.

The editorial was about the school's married student policy. I reviewed a copy of the policy after I learned that the one married student I knew would not be able to perform in a school play—just because she was married. That sounded crazy to me.

It got worse when I read the entire policy. Married students were banned from any public performance representing the high school, including theater, speech, debate, and band. They could not be publicly involved in the school's competitive athletic programs.

Married students were prohibited from speaking about married life with other students, at any time. The only person with whom they could discuss the experience of marriage was the senior guidance counselor. No offense to the deeply tenured person who held this position, but she had never been married.

My, my, this was going to be easy. All I had to do was to quote the school district policy. It was so absurd that I didn't even need to express an opinion.

The *Astor Post* was printed on an offset machine at the Columbia Press. Students prepared the writing and photographs, waxed the back of the copy, and placed each piece on a special blue-lined white cardboard sheet. As the editor, I was responsible for the layout of the opinion page: page two.

I was proud of this issue. The layout of the pages looked good. I liked my music review of *After the Gold Rush* and my editorial. I stayed late at school to make sure the paper was ready for the offset.

The next morning, my parents allowed me to drive their 1968 Malibu (yellow) to school so I could pick up the printed newspapers from the Columbia Press on the way.

At the printers, I selected a freshly run paper and opened it to admire my page two.

What the heck!

The space where my editorial was supposed to be was blank. I strode into the manager's office to complain. The high school advisor who supervised The *Astor Post* was already there.

"What happened? Did the wax fail?"

"I'm sorry, Peter. The Superintendent disapproved your editorial. He said that you couldn't criticize school board policy."

"Why didn't you tell me? I could easily have changed it so there was no criticism."

"It was his call. I'm sorry."

I loaded the papers in the car and drove to the offices of *The Daily Astorian*. I asked to speak with the editor. When I told the people at the front desk why I was there, I was granted immediate access.

The censorship of the *Astor Post* was the lead story in Astoria's daily paper, including a complete quoting of my editorial. That was far and away better circulation than the high school paper offered.

That evening, a lawyer called. He wanted to meet me the next day. I agreed to meet him at the Dairy Queen at 10 a.m.

The lawyer's firm represented a student editor who was suing their school district for censoring an opinion column. They were willing to stick with the case to the highest courts. They wanted my case as a backup if the first case had a problem.

That didn't sound like fun to me. I didn't tell anyone, but I privately figured that the school district owns the paper, so they could control the content if they want to. I was aware of another similar case litigated by the ACLU. I didn't believe that any of the cases would be successful, although the publicity might encourage some schools to delegate expressions of opinion to student editors.

I declined. I did not want to sue the school district.

The lawyer bugged me daily to reconsider.

I got calls from newspapers and radio stations, both at home and at school.

I quickly tired of this unwanted personal attention.

And I could feel the salmon clogging the river. It really seemed as if I could visualize the fish, using the extra senses that Grandpa tried to explain to me more than once.

I called Bob, and we met at the end of Erie Street.

"Let's go fishing," Bob jested.

"That's what we can do," I said, as the idea crystalized. "Let's tell our parents that this is Fall Break."

We were both in the experimental Creative Arts Program at the high school. This allowed us to miss classes as long as we told the teacher in advance and completed all of our homework. The program recognized that creative inspiration does not arrive on a schedule. We could prioritize rock 'n' roll over geometry, oil painting over world history. Fishing over journalism was probably not on the list, but I didn't intend to seek permission.

Our parents did not really understand the program, but they knew that it was something special. We could use their limited awareness to bolster our lies.

Sure enough, we told our parents that Fall Break for the Creative Arts Program began the next day, and we wanted to camp and fish at Jone's Beach. Dad offered the use of his old Ford pickup. Bob's dad offered to pick up the salmon we caught. Both sets of parents gave us cash for groceries. They happily anticipated fresh salmon!

We even had enough money left over to buy marijuana.

We drove to Jone's Beach—near Westport, Oregon. We parked the truck and lugged our tent and fishing gear down to the beach, pitched the big canvas tent, and cast our weights and lures. We stuck our fishing rods into their pole holders and clipped our bells onto the rods.

We set up a Coleman camp stove on a log that had washed up on the beach. We made coffee. We sat in folding lounge chairs and sipped.

The late-September weather was warm. One day I decided to swim out to a small island. Halfway there I glanced back at Jone's Beach. Bob was frantically jumping up and down. He yelled, but I couldn't hear a word.

Then I saw it.

I was dangerously close to a 600-foot bulk carrier headed upstream. I swam back to the beach with all the energy I could muster. Thanks, Bob!

The next week we returned to school. We faced no consequences. It seemed no one had missed us. Maybe they were glad that we were gone.

After school, we walked over to my house on Florence Avenue. No one was home. We smoked a joint in the backyard, then went up to my room. Neil Young's *Everybody Knows This is Nowhere* was on the turntable. We cranked up "Cinnamon Girl."

PERMANENT RECORD

I awoke to a creaking stair. My eyes opened as the next creak came. Slow and heavy.

It has to be Dad, I thought.

Whoever it was slowly ascended the stairs to my room as if figuring that noise is quieter when it's slow. By the time he lumbered onto the landing at the top of the stairs, I was sure it was Dad.

He entered my room.

"What's up?"

"Quiet. We don't want to wake your mother. Get your clothes on."

I went along, even though my clock said it was 3:00 a.m. What does he have in mind? There weren't good clam digging tides. We hadn't planned a fishing trip. It wasn't the high crab season when we could buy or barter for fresh Dungeness off the boats.

I followed Dad down the stairs. Outside, we got in his Ford pickup.

"Don't slam the door," he warned me.

He drove a couple of blocks to Tapiola Park, which was adjacent to Astoria High School, where I had begun my senior year. Dad recently took a job as the wood shop teacher.

He parked on a side street and got out of the pickup. I climbed out, too, groggy but curious.

Dad led us across the park to an alleyway behind the school where there was a door to the wood-shop. He selected a key from his massive keyring and unlocked the door. We entered.

Rather than switching on a light, he picked up a small flashlight that seemed conveniently placed.

Okay. Maybe he needs help moving something. But why in the middle of the night? And why doesn't he tell me what's going on? And why the flashlight?

He walked across the shop and out the door to the central atrium. I had to scramble to keep up. Now I was awake. I sensed a clandestine mission.

My senses were affirmed as he unlocked the door to the administrative offices. He pulled it closed after I was inside.

He walked to a filing cabinet as if he knew exactly where he was going. He used an oddly shaped device to release the bar that locked the filing cabinet drawers. He opened a drawer and pulled out a file which he set on a desk.

"I have to do this for you. This is your permanent file."

Dad pulled an envelope from the file and extracted the papers. I could see that the envelope was from Beaverton's Meadow Park Junior High School. I had attended Meadow Park for a couple of years.

"Here it is." He focused the flashlight on the papers.

I looked over his shoulder at a report about an incident in which I had been involved.

I started at Meadow Park in the eighth grade after I spent most of the summer with Aunt Helen and Uncle Bill in Finland and northern Europe. When we returned, I learned that my parents had moved from our home in Astoria, where I had spent my entire childhood, to Beaverton, a suburb of Portland nearly one hundred miles away.

The school year began almost immediately after I found myself in a place. I had no friends in Beaverton.

Slowly, I mustered the courage to meet people and cultivate friendships. I had experienced the start of a growth spurt over the previous months. I was taller; not so pudgy. My self-image had changed. I had confidence. I was drawn toward iconoclasts, including some tough characters that reminded me of the gangs of *West Side Story*. I tried to fit in with independent thinkers.

Leveraging their guilt for having summarily displaced their child, I prevailed on my parents to buy me a navy blue Sir Jac, a garment that was, ironically, part of an alternative culture uniform at the time.

My brother, Jack, studied at Reed College in Portland. He often seemed one step ahead of my interests, especially in books. He gave me a copy of Gandhi's autobiography, *The Story of My Experiments with Truth*. I devoured it. Soon I found utility in its precepts.

The school amended its dress code to prohibit the wearing of outer garments, including the Sir Jac, in class. I was offended at this denigration of my attire.

Meadow Park created another rule about the same time: In the cafeteria, students buying lunches were prohibited from sitting with those who brought lunches from home. Students considered the rule resoundingly ridiculous; some labeled it economic bigotry.

Drawing inspiration from Gandhi, I created a petition that asked for both the ban on jackets in class and the lunchroom seating rules to be set aside. The petition circulated quickly, with a wide variety of students gathering signatures, even the tough guys.

When nearly all of the students had signed, I presented the petition to the vice principal.

"I know exactly what to do with this," he said. Momentarily, I was heartened that this modest civil action was going to make a change.

Then, the vice principle dropped the lovingly stacked papers into his wastebasket. He ordered me back to class.

I told everyone I saw what had happened. After school, we decided to boycott the purchased lunches at the cafeteria. Everyone who was able brought food from home to share. Within a couple of days, near to no lunches were sold.

After just one week of boycott, the school administration capitulated. Free choice of seating was encouraged in the lunchroom and jackets were allowed in class.

Suddenly, I had a lot of friends.

And as it turned out, this was an incident worth documenting in my permanent school records.

☯

Dad stuffed the incident report in his coat pocket, replaced the file, locked the cabinet, and we got out of there.

I almost laughed when I realized the intent of our middle-of-the-night excursion. To me, the report was a badge of honor. I also knew that there were very likely other copies. A permanent record is not exclusive. But, hey, Dad was trying to do a good thing for me. He acted in a way that he believed would protect my future.

"Why did you take me with you?" I asked as we returned to the pickup. I was contemplating what might have happened if we had been caught, arrested, and charged with breaking and entering or something. At the very least Dad had risked his job.

"This is the way it had to be," said Dad. He pulled a bottle out from under his seat and took a slug of whiskey.

LEAP YEAR

Each month and day of 1952, a leap year, was typed on a piece of paper then sealed within one of 366 blue plastic capsules. The nearly identical capsules were placed in a large glass beaker.

On August 5, 1971, the capsules were removed from the beaker one at a time, by hand, during the televised event. The date hidden within the first capsule drawn was assigned the number one. Every male US citizen and immigrant non-citizen born on that date was also assigned the number one.

The second date drawn was assigned the number two. The process was repeated until all 366 numbers were paired with birthdates.

This was the third draft-lottery of the Vietnam War period. The lower the number assigned to a man's birthday the higher the chance that they would be drafted into military service during 1972. These people would, most likely, enter the Army's infantry.

All of the men in this lottery were either eighteen or nineteen, including me. I was assigned the number 167.

Ready or not, the young men of this period were compelled to make some serious life decisions. Some voluntarily enlisted in a branch of the military, either because they believed in the cause, or in order to choose their branch of service. Others went underground in the US or moved to another country, often Canada. Still others rendered their bodies unfit for service; removing one's big toe with a gunshot was not uncommon. Complaints of a bone spur sometimes earned a medical deferment (see Trump, D. 1968). A few refused to participate in any manner. They were imprisoned.

Two months before this lottery drawing, I had graduated from high school.

I chose not to go away to college in the fall. I wanted some life experience first, so I told myself. The reality was more like: My family couldn't help me with college expenses, and I couldn't find a way to afford, say, Stanford, even with scholarships, grants, and loans. And the lottery date approached.

I had opposed US involvement in the Vietnam War since I was twelve. I fundamentally questioned its rationale. Stopping the spread of communism by killing soldiers and suspected collaborators did not ring true. Dominos was a game, not a foreign policy. I could smell the oil in the South China Sea.

The draft was a problem. I couldn't imagine any way that I could ethically participate in the war. I didn't want to go into hiding, and I definitely was not going to shoot my toe. Prison didn't sound good, and I hadn't heard of the bone-spur gambit.

One partial solution was to register as a conscientious objector, a CO. If I could demonstrate to the draft board that I had long-standing spiritual objections to war, then, if I was drafted, I might be assigned to perform alternative non-military service or to assist the military operation in a nonviolent manner. To me, either would be better than firing a gun pointed at another human being.

How could anyone who was eighteen years old prove a sincere long-standing spiritual belief? Most of us had not lived on earth long enough to develop or test belief systems.

I had a deep reverence for life. I opposed war. I considered it barbaric. I was shocked that intelligent beings even considered war an option. I could document my beliefs. I had written about Gandhi, Buddhism, nonviolence, and the bodhisattva vow since I was thirteen or fourteen.

The draft board in Clatsop County was made up of post-draft age men from the county's communities. I'm not sure how the members of the board were selected, but they had incredible power to decide the future of young men and their families.

Before the lottery was established, they reviewed the situation of every eligible man and decided whether or not they should be compelled to serve in the military, possibly to die. Hopefully, few if any decisions were ever influenced by wealth or social position, but the lottery system was a significant equalizer. Some decisions previously made by the board were assigned to a game of chance. CO status was not among them.

I sent my draft board a ten-page hand-written letter that honestly expressed my spiritual beliefs and categorically opposed war. I also wrote that I opposed conscription as a violation of human rights. My hope was to persuade these men to invite me to a meeting, to give me an opportunity to express why I should be classified as a conscientious objector.

They did not invite me to a meeting. The draft board did support classifying me as eligible for non-military service should I be drafted through the lottery system.

Swiftly, word of my CO status traveled through the county. I didn't expect the backlash. A few times, men I knew asked me if I wanted to fight. Men I didn't know made similar requests. I managed to avoid, evade, or escape such an altercation, but I did suffer some verbal abuse. I was shocked at how polarized the people of Clatsop County had become regarding the war.

Quietly, I helped anyone who asked for assistance in making their case for CO status. I hoped my advice helped. I wasn't convinced that my Eastern Philosophy-laden letter was the tipping point for the draft board. They might have decided I was crazy or that I would be undesirable in military service. Maybe one or more of the men liked my family.

☯

Forty-one years after my birthday was paired with number 167, I sat down for a salmon lunch in a room overlooking the Columbia River. As chair of the Clatsop County Board of Commissioners, I attended a meeting that included three senior officials of the Vietnamese military. Decades ago, we might have been sworn by duty to our countries to do our best to kill each other.

These gentlemen came to the US as part of a cooperative program through which our countries share information and experience so we all can be better prepared for natural disasters.

After lunch, Americans and Vietnamese expressed gratitude for our new friendship.

JAAKO

Grandpa scoffed at the news that an astronaut had walked on the moon.

He said, "That's eastern Oregon. I've been there. They're making swimming pools with our money."

I had never heard him so worked up. I turned the newspaper article along with the photo of Neil Armstrong face down on the table.

Grandpa was in his eighties. I thought he would be thrilled to witness this historic time, this outer space event. Instead, he denied the existence of the space program, relegating Apollo 11 and Armstrong's step-walk-leap to the realm of a hoax. I had not heard of anyone else who shared Grandpa's opinion.

Maybe Grandpa had reached his limit of modernity. Sixty-odd years ago, he boarded a ship to cross the Atlantic ocean. That ship must have seemed like exotic technology to the young man from Ii, a small town tucked away in the north of Finland. New York City must have dazzled him.

He relied on the rapidly developing train system on this spacious continent to deliver him to Minnesota, where he heard that many Finns had made a new start.

Grandpa missed his connection in Chicago. For reasons unknown, he didn't get off the train to another bound for Minnesota. Whether by error or intent, he ended up in Seattle, where a porter who spoke some basic Finn steered him toward Astoria, Oregon—a bustling port at the mouth of the Columbia River.

Astoria was in the midst of an economic boom driven by the vast natural resources of the area. The supply of gargantuan logs from the temperate rainforest seemed endless. Advances in food canning technology provided the means to export the droves of salmon returning to the river system. And, there were plenty of Finns in Astoria.

He had dreamed about this place of opportunity. But he would never explain precisely why he left Finland. When I asked, he would say, "We were so poor. I had to say goodbye to my äiti." Still in his teens, he left his mother.

I studied history for clues to help me understand why he came to America.

With Finland under Russian political control at the dawn of the twentieth century, Jack Huhtaluukinen, called Jaako by his family, might soon have been conscripted to serve in the army of Nicholas II. As the youngest son, in a culture that practiced patrilineal primogeniture, wherein the family property is assumed to pass to the eldest son, he would have no wealth with which to bargain his way out of conscription.

Jaako might have been a sort of draft dodger. Perhaps he found that embarrassing.

There were other political issues with the Finns. Many subscribed to various socialist or communist philosophies, while others were drawn to nationalist thought. The expression of Finnish socialism in Astoria during the first half of the twentieth century drew backlash, both local and federal. Maybe he didn't want to take any political side, so he kept his mouth shut.

Jaako worked in the logging camps and on boats that netted salmon from the river. The boats at the time were powered by wind, with sails that suggested their fame as the Butterfly Fleet.

He was recognized for his woodworking skills and soon secured work in the shipyards, building a variety of craft.

"In Suomi, I liked to make wooden buckets. We had knives and spokeshaves," Grandpa told me. I knew Suomi meant Finland.

I drew a picture of how I imagined the pieces that made up a bucket fit against each other. Their edges needed to be beveled. The pieces measured longer on the outside than on the inside.

Grandpa was excited that I understood.

"Then I made straps to hold the boards together." He took my pencil and paper and drew another perspective that showed notches where the straps would fit.

"What were the straps made of?" I asked.

"Depends. String for a small one, metal for a big. Sometimes thin Koivu."

Birch, or Koivu, grew in abundance in northern Finland. It was common for many of the native Saami to work with birch to shape utilitarian and decorative objects.

☯

The men at the shipyards put Jaako to work on projects that required foresight and imagination. The straight planks that made up the hulls of some wooden watercraft needed to have beveled edges so they'd fit against neighboring planks, a process similar to the construction of buckets. The planks were steamed to give them flexibility, then put in forms to dry into the appropriate curvatures. But the edges of the planks were more easily shaped when dry before they went through the steaming and bending processes. Jaako had the inner vision to anticipate the constantly variable edge bevels and the comfort with hand tools to create them.

Jaako was also talented at shaping masts. A mast needed a large diameter base that narrowed to the tip. He selected the ideal straight grained wood for a mast then shaped it with hand tools—spokeshaves, planes, and calipers.

Jaako's facility with hand tools made him an obvious choice to be one the crew to build a 1950s replica of Fort Clatsop, the structure where Lewis and Clark spent the winter of 1805-06.

☯

Grandpa had an uncanny ability to see beneath the surface of rivers. I might say he could see with his mind's eye, but that wouldn't adequately describe the phenomena. It went beyond visualizing; it was more like seeing through extrasensory eyes.

He could tell where sunken trees and stumps made snags that our fishing gear might hang up on. He found the deep holes where the big Chinook salmon lurked. He organically mapped the river bottom, even in areas where dredging and winter storms made significant changes. I postulated this to be the outcome of years of experience with the currents of rivers, but I knew it was more than that.

Dad and Jack had some of Grandpa's special abilities. They often used an intuition prop: a pair of three-feet by 5/16 inch welding rods bent to an "L" shape at about six inches from the end. They held the short ends in their hands, loosely, with the long ends horizontal to the ground, parallel to each other. Then they walked in the general area where they suspected a pipe was buried in the ground. When they were over a pipe, the long ends would move, indicating the location and direction of the pipe.

I didn't believe it, so they tried an experiment: They had me use the welding rods.

It turned out that I could do it, too! It didn't matter if the pipe was a water supply line, a wastewater line, a natural gas supply line or a hose. It worked every time.

Grandpa didn't usually need anything outside of himself to accomplish similar ends. When he did, he'd find a branch and make an old-fashioned divining stick. But he didn't criticize the welding rod method.

Grandma found this water-witching useful and practical.

After all, she had her own intuition-assistant in her watch on a chain.

Most people didn't believe the reality of pipe dousing. Jack's roommate from college, Richard, did a lot of research about the subject, seeking a scientific explanation.

I just accepted that I was running with a gang of mystics.

Still, it was curious that Grandpa was so utterly cynical about the moonwalk. He categorically did not believe it happened.

He'd seen airplanes and helicopters. I was with him when we saw a blimp. But he drew the line at rocket-ships or at least at humans walking on the moon.

I picked up my newspaper. Just for fun, I accidentally on purpose gave Grandpa another peek at the moonwalk photo.

He made a sound that, if made outdoors, would be followed by a spit of tobacco juice.

ROCKPILE

The red tint of the eastern sky rapidly gave way to orange and yellow. A tender iridescence provided an ethereal backdrop to the steady Mt. Hood.

Uncle Bill fussed with his camera, a 1960s rangefinder-style Leica that he still favored. I just took in the scene, grateful that Uncle Bill drove me to work early so we could enjoy these marvelous views from Chehalem Mountain.

The day before we had arrived even earlier, and I faced the opposite direction. Uncle Bill asked me why I was not watching for the sunrise.

"I like to watch the light rush into the darker side of the sky," I said. "It can be interesting."

Uncle Bill turned around and observed the phenomena with me.

"Yes, I see," Uncle Bill exclaimed. "There must be a way to express this with photography. It's a challenge."

I agreed.

Uncle Bill liked to suggest ways to improve my photos. He often said things like, "Put some water ahead of the ship in the direction it is traveling. Give it somewhere to go."

I knew that Uncle Bill meant well when he made suggestions, even if his manner sometimes seemed arrogant. His achievements obliged him to share his knowledge. He was a wealthy businessman. He'd taken photography classes.

Although I was only twenty-one, I, too, felt a need to offer helpful hints—in this case pointing out that a special dawn of the western sky can trigger exciting connections of light, breath, and heart.

I made a mental note to dig out a ship photo in which I deliberately broke Bill's axiom. I wondered whether an interesting discussion would ensue. Of course it would, I thought. After all, it was Uncle Bill's suggestion that inspired the composition. He'd enjoy the banter.

But now Bill was eager to drive into Portland, to the offices of National Builders Hardware, the business he and Aunt Helen began and nurtured to great success.

And I had work to do.

The sun warmed the rough-plowed acreage before me, coaxing intermingling clouds of steam. It was time to pile rocks.

Cousin Mark and his wife Melody planned to grow filbert trees on this acreage, and build their dream home on the high parcel across the road. Presently, there was a small older house where Russ and Etha stayed while providing agricultural expertise. There was also an interesting blacksmith's shop, a window to the nineteenth century.

My job was to find stones amongst the clumps of overturned earth, to arrange the stones in piles, and finally, at the end of the day, to place the stones from their piles onto a flatbed that Russ pulled behind his tractor. My tools were a shovel, a pry bar, and gloves.

This was one of my favorite jobs!

Actually, there was another twist to my work: As I searched for stones, I looked out for pieces of rusty metal, farm implements from times past. These objects I put in their own piles. Russ coveted the artifacts for use in the sculpture he was creating in the blacksmith shop.

The stones were primarily basalt, scattered by the glaciers that extended through the Willamette Basin. The glaciers stretched and retreated several times during the climate twists of the Ice Ages, finally establishing in the far north and the high mountains.

Russ and Etha had spent the previous six years in India, in the Peace Corps. Russ told me he was motivated to spend time in

India after reading a US government-commissioned report that concluded that grapes would not grow in India. The authors of that study received $250,000 for reaching this conclusion. Russ and Etha found this both irritating and challenging. In India, they not only grew grapes but even made wine from their crops.

Of more personal interest to me was the collection of Indian musical instruments Russ and Etha gathered during their time in the Peace Corps. I was delighted that they let me play the tambour, the tablas, and other cultural treasures.

As each day in the field passed, it seemed the stones gained a depth of character. They spoke to my inner senses of their historic connection with lava millions of years ago, and of their relationship with the waters of streams, oceans, and skies. They revealed individual auras. My piles shined with exquisite complexity.

There are things to share and times to remain silent. These neo-psychedelic experiences seemed better kept to my own confidence, inspiring as they were.

Each night, I returned to Aunt Helen and Uncle Bill's home near Council Crest, in the hills of Portland. Aunt Helen collected carpets as she and Bill traveled around the world. She stacked them in the living room. If I hadn't been confident of the quality of the home's construction, I might have feared that the floor would collapse from the weight. Each morning and evening I hung out with those rugs; they were great company for meditation.

CHAPTER SEVEN

BEACH

ATOMIC ENERGY

Tim and I planned to hitchhike across the country playing music for subsistence, and, ultimately, roll into Key West, where we would secure employment as a musical act on a cruise ship.

We set out from Redwood City, warming our thumbs. On the first day, we made it five miles, to Stanford University. The students there had a Thanksgiving vacation street-fair going, and they were happy to provide us with a spot to play music in the sunshine. Occupants of a shared living situation called Synergy fed us and gave us an alcove to sleep and meditate. Synergy was a collection of highly intelligent vegetarian Grateful Dead fans. They lived in a former fraternity house. There was an elegant ballroom complete with a concert grand piano.

We planned a show in the ballroom. A piano-playing chemistry major wanted to join in. I composed "Circle 'Round People" during the afternoon of the show, then taught it to Tim and the pianist at our practice session. We debuted it at the show, and, happily, it filled the dance floor.

We stayed at Synergy for a week. Heck, there was no special time that we needed to be in Key West. When we felt it was time to leave, we left, clutching a contact for a place to stay at the University of California at Santa Cruz. But Tim and I didn't make it to Santa Cruz straight away.

La Honda was about thirty miles from Stanford, in the coastal mountains. It was famous—to me. It was home to Ken Kesey and the Merry Pranksters during the time chronicled in Tom Wolfe's *The Electric Kool-Aid Acid Test.*

Our first ride took us there.

Van Halen's "Runnin' With the Devil," played loud over the custom system in a red BMW piloted by a young man I imagined to be a professional surfer with an expensive haircut. He kept the tunes coming until he dropped us near La Honda, at Alice's Restaurant—a cheerful establishment named both for the proprietor, Alice, and as well as to pay homage to the Arlo Guthrie haunt.

At Alice's Restaurant, we offered to play a couple of folk songs. The manager was not only agreeable, but she also gave us lunch.

Fed, we walked down the road into La Honda proper. Suddenly, a redwood forest surrounded us. We entered a portal, a damp and ancient portal. A building from bygone era beckoned.

Apple Jack's looked to be classic dive roadhouse, with dark woodwork and dim lights. Older country folk sat at the bar and at scattered tables. When they saw our guitar cases, they asked us to play. We could play their kind of music if we chose. And we did. We made a few bucks, and they gave us a couple of beers.

"Don't go anywhere," one of our listeners implored, as he backed out the door.

Okay...

We soaked in the ambiance. After a while the man who asked us to stay returned.

"You have the gig at Boots & Saddle. But you have to come with me right now."

"What's Boots & Saddle?"

"The best damn country-rock bar in these mountains!"

Tim and I clambered into the guy's pickup. He drove deeper into the redwood portal until we came to another well-worn building.

At Boots & Saddle, they hired us to play for the night's crowd. The sound system was good and came with a house sound technician. There were good monitors on stage. This was luxurious, the best setup we had since we got to California.

We played three long sets. The energy was high, even though I felt like we were visiting an alternate dimension.

We probably shouldn't have mentioned that we were drinking Black Russians. A row of them appeared along the front of the stage, for us to imbibe at will. Neither of us had drunk alcohol lately, and I didn't even know what a Black Russian was. They were sweet and easy to drink. At the end of the evening, we felt the effects.

There we were, alone in an empty parking lot. It was raining. We didn't have a place to stay. The hours had gone by so quickly that we forgot about arranging such a nicety.

I ventured, "Why is it so cold and wet if this is California?"

"Hitchhike or find a tree?"

I was tired and inebriated. Let's find a tree.

"There are lot's of trees over there." I pointed across the road where a steep hillside was replete with redwoods.

We walked across the road and climbed the hill.

"One place is as bad as another," Tim said. He rolled out his sleeping bag.

I did the same and crawled in fully clothed.

The ground was already soaked. The rain poured. I wondered if it was possible that we might drown. We'd made the wrong choice.

Wearing our wet packs, carrying our guitars in their cases, dragging our soaked sleeping bags, we stumbled onto the shoulder of the dark road.

A car stopped. The young woman inside rolled down her window.

"Get in."

"But we're wet."

"That's why you need to get in."

We did.

Carrie drove back in the direction of Apple Jack's. She took a side road into a neighborhood of modular homes, and double-wide and single-wide trailers. Carrie explained that she had just left her husband. She was going to her mother-in-law's place.

When we arrived, she helped us get our saturated world into a mobile home. Carrie and her mother-in-law, Angie, rang out our sleeping bags in a laundry basin. They put one in a large drier. They gave us towels and blankets and insisted that we take off all our clothes. Soon, there was a meal of eggs, potatoes, and toast.

It was as if they did this sort of thing every night.

They otherwise ignored us, as they sat at a small table and complained to each other about Ron—the husband and son. I considered the possibility that Ron might be upset, that he might have a gun, but I was very sleepy.

When I awoke, our bags were dry. Our clothes were dry, too. We put some on and arranged our packs, gushing with gratitude.

"It's what people do," explained Carrie.

She took us to the highway, then sped back home to her husband. Ron had apparently made adequate promises over the phone.

Soon we had a ride. We were on our way to the California coast. Our driver let us out at Bonny Doon beach.

We had passed through the other end of the dark portal. It was sunny. It was a beach. Let's check it out.

We climbed over a dune. Cliffs bookended the small, nearly deserted beach. Vegetation topped the cliffs; perhaps some sort of crop?

Gentle, regular waves caressed the sandy beach. The sound mesmerized. I plopped my pack on the sand and leaned against it. My reverie flowed into meditation and a little nap.

When consciousness returned to my eyes, and they opened, I was amazed at the huge pile of firewood that Tim had gathered without disturbing me. He had even created a stone fire-ring. He ignited the assemblage in the ring as soon as he noticed I was awake.

Santa Cruz was a short way down the road, but this was a nice place. We had tea and prepared a vegetarian meal. The sand was like a delightful mattress that automatically adjusted to the shape of our bodies.

In the clear dawn, I stood to stretch. About fifty feet away,

I spied two additional filled sleeping bags.

Tim set off a warming fire that featured loud snaps and cracks. Sharon and April came over to request spots by the fire.

"Welcome," said Tim. "Are you on vacation?"

"Not exactly," said Sharon—mid-twenties, slim, straight blonde hair. Soon to be straightforward?

"We're driving for surprises," said April, who was round and bubbly, and about the same age as Sharon. "We both lost our jobs, so we filled up Sharon's car and left Sacramento in the rear-view mirror. We think those are Brussels sprouts on the hill." She pointed at a cliff.

I wasn't quite awake. Tim was. He said, "Why don't you and April go get some Brussels sprouts and Sharon and me, we'll make coffee."

The climb was steep, but not unreasonable. April was giddy when she saw the endless rows of plants, each bearing dozens of multi-sized sprouts. This was not my favorite vegetable, but I was, nonetheless, complicit in the theft of a couple stems.

Tim cheered for the Brussels sprouts. Well, okay, I thought, if it makes him happy. He poured me a cup of coffee.

Tim boiled the sprouts to not-too-tender perfection, distributed them in four plastic bowls, and offered salt and butter to all.

My sister, Jane, talked me into trying Brussels sprouts a couple of times. I had never been thrilled at their taste or texture. But this was different. Stolen sprouts on a chilly morning, with salt and butter...wow, this might be my favorite food!

☯

Every cubic inch of Sharon's sedan was stuffed with household goods and bags of chips and cookies, but we squeezed in. Sharon and April deposited us in Santa Cruz.

April was crushed that we wouldn't invite her to go to Key West with us.

In 1978, Santa Cruz was a perfect town for traveling minstrels like Tim and me. There were abundant locations to play and stay. But, for us, this would be a short visit.

The poster on a light pole jumped out at both of us. The Atomic Energy Commission was holding hearings about whether they should permit the Diablo Canyon Nuclear Power Plant at Avila Beach, near San Luis Obispo. We had something to say about that. It felt like a purpose.

We had three days to get to Avila Beach. Based on our recent rate of travel, we'd better get going. After a night in a church in downtown Carmel and an ocean-front slumber in San Simeon, we found ourselves in a Volkswagen van with a group from Berkeley also on the way to the Diablo Canyon hearing.

The sheet to sign-up to testify before the Atomic Energy Commission was filled with nuclear scientists and people with initials after their names. What could we say, in a mere two minutes each, that could possibly persuade the Commission to withhold a license for this nuke? I stared blankly at the sheet.

"We'll sing a song," said Tim. As always, he was quick with an idea.

"What song?"

Tim got the attention of one of AEC staff and asked, "How long will it be before we're called to testify? Can we combine our two-minutes, so we have four minutes total?"

"About twenty minutes. You can testify together."

Tim signed our names to the sheet and answered my question.

"The song we're going to write."

We sat in the sun on a grassy hill, pens in hands. I wrote the verses and Tim the chorus to "No Queremos el Diablo." We agreed on an arrangement and returned to the hearing room with minutes to spare. We were in tune.

As we completed the debut of our new song, the room erupted with applause. The anti-nuke people treated us like heroes. They hauled us back to the Cal Poly dorms. The students helped arrange gigs for us in the local clubs.

In a couple of days, we ended up with our own rooms in a house in Los Osos, rooms we could use while the usual student occupants were home on December break.

On my birthday, December 30, we were back on the road. The next segment of our adventure took us twenty-three miles. We slept in a frosty park in Arroyo Grande.

THREE RAINBOWS

We woke up early on a sunny January morning, in San Diego's Balboa Park. Tim and I had no plans for the day. We quietly rolled up our sleeping bags and re-arranged our packs.

"Let's go up by the garden that we saw yesterday," said Tim.

"Sure," I replied. "That's a nice place. But there aren't many blooms."

"I was thinking about the little outdoor building. The acoustics might be good. I'd just like to play for us, for fun, instead of trying to get tips or working at that dive bar."

That does sound refreshing. I agreed. "Pergola."

"What?"

"It's called a pergola—the building that's open to the gardens at Marston House. Yeah, let's go there."

Tim was right. The wooden pergola had nice acoustics. Playing just for fun revealed some starts for new songs. And I'd never heard Tim's little Martin sound better.

"Maybe we should find a spot to set up closer to the zoo," I suggested. We could probably earn some tips in the more crowded part of the park.

"Maybe later."

After a bit, a neatly dressed young man walked up. He smiled and said, "Please do not to stop playing." He gave a little clap when we finished whatever song we were doing.

"That's nice," he said. His voice was soft and sincere. "Do you know any songs by Arthur Lee?"

I knew some, but I doubted that Tim did. Arthur Lee's

band, Love, was one of my favorite groups. "Signed, DC" was simple enough. I looked at Tim. He could deal with it, I was certain. I went right into the song.

Our guest seemed happy. After the song, he thanked us with a hint of sadness. He placed a fifty-dollar bill and a Snow Seal in my guitar case. He pulled a leather holder out of his wallet and removed a business card.

He put the card in my case, looking straight into my eyes, and said, "Call me if you want to make a record." He walked away.

I looked at the card. Wow.

"Who was that," asked Tim.

"That was Arthur Lee."

☯

Twenty years later, I rode with Leon Hendrix in the back of Henry Lewis' forest-green 1976 Jaguar limousine.

Almost randomly, I asked, "Did you ever meet Arthur Lee?"

"Oh yeah. We were friends. He was there when Jimi's star got put on Hollywood Boulevard. He was about the only person there that I could relate to." Leon looked at the limo's ceiling. "We got out of there and went to his apartment. I disappeared for two weeks. We had a party."

Leon climbed forward in the limo. "Henry, stop up there at the rib place. I want to teach Peter about collard greens." He turned back to me. "Collard greens are my secret. That's how I stay young."

He did look young for fifty. He was thin and agile, with long curly hair and rose glasses. Okay, I'll give him the look of a thirty-nine-year-old. Appearances aside, Leon was about six years younger than his older brother Jimi Hendrix would have been—had Jimi lived.

Leon overflowed with emotion-laden stories about his childhood, and about precious times with Jimi. They grew up in Seattle, in the projects and other modest housing, primarily with their father, Al. Leon also bounced around in the foster-care system.

Jimi was Leon's hero, like my brother, Jack, was mine. Leon loved to tell stories of Jimi's courage. He vividly recalled freezing up on a train trestle. Jimi knocked him from the path of a speeding train—just in time.

One summer day, Leon nearly drowned in the Green River. Going under for the final time, he saw a golden glint. Later, he realized this was the sun reflected off the house-key that Jimi kept on a string around his neck; it caught his eye as his big brother jumped in and saved him.

As a young adult, Leon had some difficulties with the legal system. As United States involvement in the Vietnam War intensified, Leon and many other young men were offered a choice between prison and the army. Leon chose the army. However, he sincerely objected to the war. And he didn't take it well when those of superior rank told him what to do.

When the Jimi Hendrix Experience came to Seattle, Jimi sent a car to fetch Leon from the military base. Leon couldn't bring himself to return to army life, so the absent-without-leave brother joined the entourage of his rockstar sibling. Leon landed for a time at the Beverly Hilton, in the late-60s world of parties, celebrities, and groupies.

At one point, for no reason he could explain to me at the time, Leon flew to Seattle. The police greeted him on arrival. He was arrested and sent to the state prison at Monroe, Washington. He never saw his beloved brother again.

☯

The collard greens were delicious.

Henry loaded us back into the limo as it started to sprinkle. He took us to Renton to visit Jimi's grave.

Henry Lewis was an interesting man. He once played minor league baseball in Portland, Oregon, where they called him "Fireball." For several years he managed Peters Habit, a popular Portland nightclub where he got to know many prominent Oregonians—including Governor Tom McCall.

In Seattle, Henry operated a bail bonds business. That's how Henry met Leon. Leon or one or more of his nine children occasionally needed to make bail. Henry became a family friend.

"Hey, Peter, look at that!" Leon pointed out the window at a rainbow. "Jimi said that there are always three rainbows if you look close enough."

By gosh, there were three rainbows.

Henry manipulated his limo along the narrow roads through the cemetery.

"Here it is." Leon almost jumped out of the car.

Fans took turns making rubbings of the inscription on Jimi's fairly modest stone. One brought his Stratocaster to bump against the stone.

They looked up at Leon, and one recognized him. Soon, I operated three cameras so the fans could have their photos taken with Jimi's little brother.

"Janie and Al are planning something big over there," said Leon.

Leon and Jimi's father, Al, re-married, after the passing of the boys' mother, Lucille. Al's new wife had a daughter, Janie, who he adopted. Now, she ran the Experience Hendrix corporation and controlled the financial side of Jimi's artistic legacy.

"I wish they'd do something for our mother. You know, she's here, too. Her marker is just a can." Leon led me into an older part of the cemetery. "It's over here."

Some markers looked like cans, but, that day, we couldn't find Lucille Jeter among them.

BRAWLEY

A miserable chilly Southern California rain had Tim and me pinned. After hitching a ride out of El Cajon, we ended up at the Alpine overpass of the Kumeyaay Highway.

It was one of those humid downpours that soak your clothes within minutes of exposure. The car we'd been riding in took off down Tavern Road to a luxury home on five acres, with a view to Mexico. The driver relished describing his property to us, as he took regular swigs off a flask he said contained Patron tequila.

Now that we were outside of a car, darkness made the unrelenting rain more ominous.

We'd begun the day's journey in a rough patch of downtown San Diego. For the past week, we performed as the musical duo Cowboy and Junior on the catwalk of Jim Jones Sound Gallery. We happened upon the opportunity when we stopped by looking for a place to play. Fortunately, I guess, for us, the nightclub temporarily lost their license to display nude females on that catwalk. They hired us on the spot.

The pay wasn't enough to upgrade our housing, which was a eucalyptus grove in Balboa Park.

Ironically, we left San Fransisco not long after the Jonestown Massacre. The establishment where we worked had nothing to do with the mass suicide/murder perpetrated by a man named Jim Jones, but it was still weird.

It was January 1979. We were awesome musicians, but most of our audience—comprised of young sailors and aficionados of cheap beer— didn't notice.

Tim was a six-foot-four bearded redhead music major from Wisconsin. We met when he showed up in Astoria. We became fast friends and enjoyed jamming on our acoustic guitars. We both wrote songs.

A friend gave me a ride from Astoria to San Francisco, where I intended to give myself a month-long vacation. I rode into the city on November 19, as the newspaper hawkers held up headlines about Jonestown.

In San Francisco, I cultivated a routine which involved drinking coffee and writing stream-of-consciousness poetry at the storied Psalms Cafe, the site of a former drug store, on the corner of Haight and Ashbury.

One morning Tim walked in. I was surprised but feigned that I was expecting him, just to see his amazed expression. We were both traveling with our guitars.

"Let's go busking," Tim suggested. "We can check out the place where they turn the cable cars around."

He wanted us to play our guitars and sing on the street, for tips. That sounded like something I could tell my future grandchildren about.

When we got to the suggested place, other musicians had already set up camp. So we wandered over to Fisherman's Wharf and found an agreeable spot.

Whoa Howdy! In a couple of hours, we had two-hundred bucks. We repeated this feat daily, having a serious blast.

Then, Mayor George Moscone and Commissioner Harvey Milk were murdered at city hall. The mood of the city was bleak.

Tim and I had a meeting.

"Let's go to Key West," said Tim.

"Why?" I replied. "Where is Key West?"

"South Florida. Ernest Hemingway and all that. They have cruise ships there that go all around the Caribbean. We'll get a job playing music on a cruise ship."

"Is that how it works? We just show up and get hired?"

"We'll probably have to audition, but that's no problem.

We're writing original songs, and we play well. People like us."

And I thought it was our hats and overalls.

"We can practice on the way there."

"How will we get there?" I ventured. Plane? Train?

"Hitchhike."

Of course.

Tim had a 000-18 Martin guitar from 1957. It had fantastic action and tone. When Tim plugged into an amp, it sounded like an electric guitar. With a slide, he evoked the spirit of Duane Allman.

I took a breath. I had a woodworking business, but not a job to go home to. I was recently divorced. Dad had died in June.

Why not!

☯

We could have extended our employment at Jim Jones Sound Gallery, but it was getting testy in Balboa Park. It seems a serial killer was chopping off the limbs of people who camped in the park.

Ingrid worked at a restaurant across the street from the Sound Gallery. I went there to drink coffee. Her work outfit was simple—nude. She was attractive in a thin, blonde, and pale way. She had a matter-in-fact presence that saved me from getting too distracted by her nudity while I enjoyed my coffee.

"I heard you last night," she said. "You can do better than that dump."

"I'd like to."

She wrote down the address of a place in El Cajon, a big club with a dance floor and a house sound system. We quit our job and took the bus to El Cajon.

There was no work at the club for a duo. They wanted bands with drums and bass, especially in the country-punk genre. It was a no go.

It was getting dark. Neither of us was into backtracking. We walked to the freeway on-ramp and pointed toward Key

West.

☯

At the crest of a coastal mountain pass in almost-Mexico, we got soaked with nowhere to play.

We searched for a tree for shelter, but they didn't have that sort of trees. The only dry place was under the overpass. The highway people must have seen this coming. The sides beneath the overpass sloped at a steep angle from near the top right down to the pavement of Tavern Road. We could prop ourselves up high on the slope with our knees bent, but if we dozed off, we'd tumble down onto the road. Damn.

We sat there, damp but not getting wetter, sleepy but compelled to avoid sleep.

Hands around his knees, Tim sighed. I nodded. It was eerily quiet, desolate. In the haunting darkness, a can blew onto the pavement below us. It rattled as it zigzagged back and forth, taking its own sweet time to get to the other side. We were fortunate men that night: If we weren't there, we never would have heard the rattles of that can. It was the loneliest sound in the universe, so strange and beautiful.

At first light, we dragged ourselves onto the shoulder of the freeway, a little past the sign that purported to prohibit hitchhiking. We got a ride right away.

I sat in front. The dawning sun warmed my face. The long straightaway descended at a nearly constant angle from the pass to lowlands that looked like a desert to me. Our benefactor dropped us at the intersection with Highway 111. He was heading north.

Instead of continuing east we chose to try for a ride going south to Mexicali. A taste of Mexico would be fun. Out with the thumbs. The first car picked us up! The man and woman in the front seat asked us about our plans. Tim told them about Key West. He rambled on about our recent exploits.

"That sounds like an adventure," said the woman. "You

know it's probably not a good idea to cross over to Mexico right now. There have been some problems."

There was no time to get additional elucidation. We got out in the California border town—Calexico—where we spent the night on a stage in an empty public park. In the morning, we played music on the stage, not aware that we had an audience of one. Dusty, a young truck driver, overheard our performance.

When we finished a song, someone was clapping. Dusty came out from behind a bush.

"Bravo!"

We headed back north in Dusty's truck. He chose an intersection to drop us off.

Dusty needed to take his truck into El Centro to get some work done on it. He suggested that we continue on to nearby Brawley, where we should check out the bar at the Hotel Dunlack. They sometimes had live music.

"It's easy to get rides around here," said Dusty.

He was right. A pickup with a tall make-shift canopy pulled over for us shortly after I stuck out my thumb. We got in back with a crowd that already seemed to fill the space to capacity. They generously made room for us. At the outskirts of Brawley, we all got out. The truck sped back toward Mexico.

As we walked through Brawley, an older woman ran out and handed us each a grapefruit.

"Gracias," said Tim.

I approximated a similar sound of appreciation.

The woman used the Spanish language to persuade us to wait. Soon a very old, very wrinkled man arrived. He said nothing as he led us to the railroad tracks. There he made some gestures that seemed to mean that he belonged on one side of the tracks and we should stick to the other. He also pointed out a large building on the side of the tracks reserved for the likes of us: Hotel Dunlack.

Smiles for all. We waved as we crossed the tracks.

Several men were drinking in the bar at the Hotel Dunlack. We asked if we could play a couple of songs.

"Sure, you can play," said the bartender. "Maybe one of these fellers will give you a tip."

"Or the boot," said one of the patrons.

They all laughed.

We played Tim's new song called "Reckless and Abandon."

They liked it. One of those in our audience was the owner.

"Look," said the owner. "We need a band for the weekend. The regular band quit. Can you start tonight."

"What's the pay?"

Tim kicked me.

"Two-hundred-fifty a night." He looked at our backpacks. "And a free room at the hotel."

Sold.

The room was on the second floor. The Hotel Dunlack had been elegant at one time, but not anymore. Ragged carpet covered the stairs, the landing, and the broad hallway of floor two. The room smelled of mold from the Wild West. We had to screw a bulb into the ancient ceiling fixture to turn on the light.

It sure beat the wet and sleepless night at Alpine.

The first night went great. The bar was packed. The sound system was simple but adequate. The owner was pleased, and he spoke of inviting us to be the house band.

The second night was a bit more difficult.

At 7:30 we took our guitars and walked down the wide hall to the stairway. Someone was yelling on the landing. When we got there, we found a man with a knife stuck in his chest. He cursed in multiple languages as he bled.

The owner arrived.

"Don't worry," he said. "I can handle this. Just go on downstairs and play."

The show went okay, but I kept thinking about the angry stabbed man.

A stout and persistent drunk implored us to let him play harmonica with us. Tim finally relented and handed him a harp. We played a couple of songs, but he didn't fit in. We took a break. The drunk and his friend walked out through the back door of the bar with Tim's harmonica.

I followed them out the door and into an alley. I asked for the harmonica. My guitar was still strapped around my neck.

They turned around. The player put one hand behind my neck and prepared to smash me in the face with the other.

"Give him the harmonica," boomed a nearby voice in the alley. Dusty, the truck driver, stood pointing a substantial looking pistol at my would-be assailant. In an instant, I had the harmonica in my hand.

Dusty and I walked back into the bar. I tried to get Tim's attention, but he was distracted by a young lady.

I was pleased with the retrieval of the harmonica, even though my stupidity might well have steered the situation to a different outcome.

Tim finally turned our way.

"Dusty helped me save your harp, Tim."

"That's okay. I let that guy use the one with a blown reed. I was gonna throw it away."

SNOWBIRD

Snowbird ran out of gas in downtown Laguna Beach, California. It felt to me as if the 1957 Ford had nearly accomplished her mission.

The car came to Tim and me after we made a significant decision about our journey across the United States. We reversed course at Tucson.

Tucson was generally good to us. We easily found cafes and bars near the University of Arizona where we could play our music. The street people were friendly. We joined with a few who crashed in an abandoned warehouse. Vegetarian lunch was available for a dollar apiece at the Sikh temple. We even had the opportunity for international travel.

We had made friends with a small band of itinerate musicians and friends who lived in a converted school bus. One day we joined them on an adventure. We took the school bus to the Mexican border, then walked across into Nogales—four disheveled minstrels and their acoustic guitars, and their entourage, all sporting faded colors.

Children surrounded us as we entered the country, seeking dollars and demanding that we play music for them. My attention was drawn to an emaciated woman who sat on the sidewalk and raised a single arm so thin it appeared amazingly long. Her still-elegant hand tipped back beyond ninety degrees. I placed a precious dollar in her hand. She voiced appreciation with a dry, dehydrated sound. Her piercing yet gentle eyes told a deep, true story.

By the time we reached the town plaza, we had gathered a large following that expected to become our audience. We pulled our guitars out of their cases to perform for a crowd that exceeded fifty. Soon coins and colored paper littered our cases.

After a few songs, a local law enforcement officer arrived. He was short with a round abdomen. He explained that we needed to buy a permit to play in the plaza. Tim asked him where we could get a permit and how much would it cost. The officer said that we needed to go to the main police station, except it was closed right now for siesta time. Fortunately, he could take care of the permit, for a modest fee.

Several of our fans overheard this discussion. They surrounded the officer and moved en masse away from us. Townspeople encouraged us to play. So we did.

After our song, the ever-growing audience clapped and yelled appreciation. The rotund officer was encouraged to come up to us. He put a handful of cash in my open case. He told Tim that no permit would be necessary after all.

The locals let us know about a large bar where we might negotiate an opportunity to perform that evening. I wanted to explore a bit, so I wandered off by myself, arranging to meet Tim later.

As I walked by a shop that appeared to specialize in liquors, the shopkeeper popped out and asked me to play a song. I obliged and quickly drew a small crowd. The shopkeeper asked for more. I agreed but requested a bottle of tequila in exchange for three songs. He agreed, requesting The Beatles. For the third song, I played "Eight Days a Week." I walked off with a smattering of Mexican coins and a fifth of Mezcal.

We ended up with a gig at the large bar—a crowded, rowdy scene. A trumpet player who said his name was Kilo joined us for a few tunes. He wasn't bad. At the break, a few locals ran up to me. They said, "Don't deal with Kilo. He is Federale."

I appreciated their kindness and made a mental note never to buy marijuana in Mexico from anyone named Kilo.

In the wee hours, we crossed back into the United States, passing an easy border check. After we were in the States, we noticed a Mexican woman with her children having difficulty with her Volkswagen bug. Tim and I gave the car a push, an act that ended with us back in Mexico. I considered going back to the crossing guards to explain why we were back, but it just seemed too complicated. We turned and ran back to the USA, without incident.

Rodeo time was coming to Tucson. We had stashed enough money to rent a couple of couches in the South Tucson barrio. We landed an afternoon spot at a bar across from the rodeo grounds, as well as a regular late-night slot at a rock 'n' roll club in the barrio. After five straight days of this, both Tim and I lost our voices.

Yeah, we lost our voices, and we lost our resolve. Portland seemed like a dream destination. I wanted to be there as soon as possible.

"Let's go to the airport," said Tim, with what was left of his voice.

"Why would we want to do that?"

"We can hitch a ride on a plane."

That sounded crazy enough to be realistic. We clambered to the highway and stuck out our thumbs. Then we walked for a while. We stuck them out again. No luck.

So we made a decision: One of us would hitchhike heading east, the other heading west. If we got a ride to the airport, that would be a sign that we should hitch a flight. If we got a ride going east, we would press on toward Florida. If a car going west stopped, we would head back to California and points beyond.

Almost immediately a westbound car stopped for me. Tim ran across the highway to join us. The ride took us all the way to Tempe, right to Arizona State.

It was a pleasant sunny afternoon. A small concrete platform on the park-like grounds of the university beckoned. We played a few instrumentals, really just goofing off. A handful of young people stopped to listen.

The crowd grew a bit, including a couple of people with video equipment. We stopped playing; our fans wandered off. We had the makings for cheese and red onion sandwiches and assembled them. Then we leaned against our packs on our adopted platform. We both dozed off.

"Excuse me. Hello?"

I opened my eyes. A slender, neatly dressed older man, with short hair, was examining us.

"Uh, we were having lunch," I ventured. Were we about to get kicked off the campus?

"I saw you on TV, on the four o'clock news show."

Tim was awake now. He looked at me as if I might have an explanation. I didn't.

"On TV? When?"

"Just now. I mean I saw you, and I ran down here hoping you were still around. I live really close."

I checked my intuition. Pervert? Nutcase? Serial killer?

He cleared part of my concerns, saying, "I'm a professor here." Still, he could have avocations.

Tim was now engaged. "Were we on TV today?" he said.

"Yes," said the professor. "You both seem to have some problems with your voices."

We decided to trust him for now. The professor took us back to his home, a nice mid-century rambling ranch where Frank Lloyd Wright might have felt at home. Our friend gave us bedrooms. He offered to do our laundry. He encouraged us to take showers. He made dinner—with salmon from the Columbia River!

I awoke with the sun and reviewed my memories of the day before. The last part didn't make sense, or did it? My room smelled clean. So did I. Maybe everything was fine. I fell back asleep.

When I awoke the next time, I noticed a neat pile of my clothes, cleaned. I put them on and opened my door, with only a small expectation of encountering a madman with a knife. No one was in the hall, but I could hear guitars in the distance. I followed the sound and discovered Tim and the professor slowly strumming chords. They noticed me and stopped.

"Tim is giving me a lesson."

Aha! Perchance we've been abducted as slaves to provide musical education?

"I bet you're hungry."

It turned out that the professor was a genuinely nice man. He liked our music, especially Tim's version of bluegrass. He took care of us, nursing our throats back to health. Once we could sing, he played our manager, getting us into coffee shops and other small venues. We actually had some notoriety from our brief candid appearance on local TV.

One of the odder gigs the professor arranged was at a Round Table pizza place. There was no stage. Somehow, Tim talked me into standing on a small round table with my guitar while he mounted an adjacent table. Dangerous, but it went over well.

At the break, two men in our audience were trying to sell their car. I listened as the offering price dropped from $300 to $200 to $150. At that point I jumped in, "I'll take it if you'll give it to me for free."

"Sold!"

The men were heading off on a six-month bicycle tour of Mexico, especially the Yucatan Peninsula. In the morning the professor took us to meet the bike riders at the motor vehicle department.

Snowbird, as we called the 1957 Ford, was blue and white, with Colorado plates. Her headliner boasted strung monofilament fishing line holding up dozens of comic books. Her bumper sticker implored, "Support Your Local Police, and Keep Them Independent."

With the car, it was easy to return to wanderlust. We bid adieu to the professor and pointed Snowbird north. Our intended destination was Chicago, where we planned to surprise Tim's brother, the president of a motorcycle gang.

Just south of Flagstaff, ten-foot piles of snow framed the highway. Maybe Chicago would not be so easily assessable.

Snowbird took us to the new sports arena at Northern Arizona University. We walked in like the place had been built for us. Tim crashed on a bench. I wrote additional verses to a song I had begun writing in San Francisco, "One Eye Open."

We rolled through Sedona, Jerome, Prescott, and Yuma, on our way to California. I confessed my love of sun.

We turned off the Kumeyaay Highway at the Alpine overpass to pay homage to travelers that only a few months prior had spent a miserable rainy night at this place.

For each of us, there was no doubt about our destination: Laguna Beach.

LAGUNA BEACH

They called the neighborhood the Top of the World. The houses were big; many of the views expansive. High above the oceanfront and the village of Laguna Beach, it felt heady, even otherworldly.

"Turn right coming up, then go down that driveway," directed Fish. "You got it, Davie."

Dave and I ran into Fish near Main Beach. Fish was the bass player in Reckless and Abandon, my group from 1979.

Fish suggested that we go in on a quarter ounce of marijuana that he could get for eighty dollars. Why not?

As Dave maneuvered his hand-painted, bright-yellow pickup through the Top of the World, I noticed a house I had been to before.

In 1979, Tim and I rolled into Laguna Beach in our 1957 Ford, Snowbird. We pushed her into a parking place since we'd run out of gas. We walked around the charming village until we came to a bar called Mothers. We carried our guitars because there was not a way to properly secure the Ford.

"Do you play those?" challenged the tall, thin woman behind the bar.

"We sure do," flirted Tim.

"Do you know any Billy Holiday," she replied.

"I'm not sure," said Tim, "but we can figure it out."

"My name is Alice."

I jumped in, "I'm Peter, and this is Tim."

Alice brought out a guitar case and extracted a weathered Martin. She recently returned to Laguna Beach after spending a dozen years in Las Vegas playing and singing torch blues and Willie Nelson-style country.

The bar was empty save for us, and Alice invited us to play. The guitars and voices, especially Alice and Tim's, blended beautifully. On the spot, we vowed to form a band.

Alice laughed when we told her that we called ourselves Cowboy and Junior on our road trip. She laughed more when we told her about our plan to get hired as a band on a cruise ship.

We called the new band Reckless and Abandon, after one of Tim's songs. Alice helped find Scott, an extraordinary drummer and a talented chef of French cuisine. Through another friend of Alice's, we found Fish, a long-time LA studio musician.

Tim and I had played together every day for over a year. Our musical connection was nearly telepathic. With Alice, Scott, and Fish we had an exciting five-piece.

We met a few young women of the Laguna Beach police department during rehearsals for a band-promoted show at the Women's Center. The police officers volunteered to respond to noise complaints, only to hang out and dance to our music.

We gained some popularity but weren't making much money. Tim and I earned a few bucks through a local day labor program. One assignment sent us to the Top of the World to do some gardening.

The folks that hired us rented a home in the neighborhood. One was a doctor; the other a surveyor. They were planning a party and wanted the grounds to look cared for. We did a great job on the first day, and they had us back the next morning.

Talking with us the second day, the roommates learned that we were musicians. On the spot, they hired us to play for their party— that night. Scott and Fish were not available, but Alice could do it. She got off work just in time.

I left a note for Alice letting her know that our gig was for a toga party. I suggested that she might dress up in divine decadence. I knew she had some fun outfits.

Togas abounded at the sprawling house. We were set up and ready to play when Alice arrived, looking stunning. She stepped to her mic, covered it to set off just enough feedback to get the partiers' attention, and said, "Good evening. We're Divine Decadence."

She led us off with "Body and Soul" and never looked back. At the break, we gathered several $100 tips, and we were offered access to a smorgasbord of recreational and pharmaceutical chemicals laid out on a table. Tim and I declined. Alice nursed her flask of Southern Comfort.

By the end of the second set, the toga-clad were throwing each other into the pool. For the last set, Alice avoided words, and Tim took extended solos. The music matched the decadence of the party.

In the end, we realized that we now had two groups: Reckless and Abandon and Divine Decadence.

☯

David and I sat in the truck while Fish went to the door of the house. The man who answered the doorbell waved for us to come in. Once we were inside, he introduced himself as Eric—the great, great grandson of President Taft. For whatever reason, he informed us that he was the only one home. He invited David and me to sit at a glass-top dining table with a distant ocean view.

"Not you, Mr. Fish," said Eric. "You move over here by the hall. And get on your knees." He pointed a pistol at Fish to enforce his requests. David and I were perfectly positioned in Eric's line of sight to make sure we didn't try to assist Fish.

Eric accused Fish of stealing a gun from a party the weekend before. Fish denied it and begged for his life. They went back and forth. Fish pointed out that he had come back to the house.

"Why would I come here if I stole a gun?"

"From what I hear you do a lot of stupid things."

"Let me leave. I'll never come back here again. You don't

want a mess."

"Right. I don't want a mess. Get out of here. Run. Run. Run, Mr. Fish."

Fish ran right out the front door. He never looked back.

Eric closed the door and turned his attention to David and me. He said, "I was just about to make Pina Coladas." He set the firearm on the table and poured ingredients into a nearby blender. The gun was closer to me than it was to him, but he might have another gun. I stayed in my chair.

Eric served up the drinks. "What do you boys do?"

"We play music," said David.

"I can help you with your careers," exclaimed Eric, excitedly. "My friends have the best club in town—the Boom Boom Room." He looked us over.

"Are the drinks okay?"

"Perfect," I said. It's a good thing I liked Pina Coladas.

The gun was still on the table. David watched the view.

Eric mused, "I probably should have killed him. He deserves to die. But he was right: I didn't want to clean up a mess. The house is looking so good." He laughed.

Looking us over again, Eric said, "We'll need to get your hair done. You'll look really good. How does that sound?"

David chimed in, "That sounds really good. Thank you."

"I'll call my hairdresser right now. We can have you singing at the Boom Boom tonight."

David continued, "That is so sweet of you, but we have a special appointment this evening. Could we do it another time?"

"A special appointment. That sounds important. And mysterious. Well, drink up. You don't want to be late." He laughed. "Late!"

We drank up and started to get up. Eric put his hand on the gun. "Why did you come here? What do you want?"

"We were just looking for a quarter," I said.

"That's no problem." He picked up the gun and opened a drawer in a sideboard. He took out a bag and left the gun in the drawer. He closed the drawer and tossed the bag to me. "Here you go. On the house." Then he opened the drawer again. He took out a card and handed it to David. "You call me when you're ready to be a star."

We walked out of the house and got in the truck. Eric smiled and waved.

CASUAL LABOR

The sooner you got to casual labor, the more likely you were to be hired. That was the conventional wisdom about the day labor center in Laguna Beach, in 1978. In my experience, it was more convoluted than that.

It's true if you got there by seven, you'd have a better chance to hook up with a contractor who would keep you for a full day. My friend, Stan, preferred to work as many hours as possible each day, as long as he didn't have to promise to work for any one person for more than one day. The seven o'clock group was fine for Stan. He also liked working with concrete. I didn't.

Tim and I enjoyed weeding for Leonard. Leonard showed up with his van, just before eight. He quickly selected four people and waved the group into the van. He handed each of us a bag with a bagel, cheese, a banana, and a packet of jelly. Four styrofoam cups of black coffee were already strategically placed in cup holders in the van.

Leonard was a short, thin, middle-aged man, with a smattering of curly dark hair. He contracted with office building managers to keep their landscapes tidy, or at least relatively free from weeds. Noteworthy, his services were herbicide-free.

We devoured our breakfasts as Leonard followed Laguna Canyon Road to the mini-malls of El Toro. He dropped us off, one at a time, at our morning weed patches, equipped with gloves, biodegradable bags, and a couple of hand tools.

At about 11:45 Leonard returned for us. Each cupholder now held a bottle of a fruit juice from Laguna Beach Juice Company. He handed each of us sixteen dollars and dropped us off at Main Beach.

It worked out fine. We had food money. We were on the beach by noon with the whole day ahead. We wrote, played music, and philosophized with other drifters. I swam in the ocean nearly every day. Tim never dipped a toe in salt water.

We slept in an abandoned house a short way out the Laguna Canyon. A fun colony of Jesus Freaks shared the space.

One morning when we arrived at Casual Labor, an older woman walked up to me and asked, "Do you paint?"

I did. I could. I might. When I was a cabinetmaker in Oregon, I usually hired someone to do the necessary painting. But I certainly could paint. When I was ten, Grandpa put a huge paintbrush in my little hand and sent me up a ladder to where he had used a metal coat hanger to suspend a bucket of paint. That summer I helped to paint my grandparents' house.

"Outside or in?" I asked.

"What?"

"I can paint exteriors and interiors."

"I knew that when I saw you, of course," she said. "What is your hourly fee?"

I stumbled. It was thirty-five back home. I said, "Seven-fifty." Quite a few competitors were waiting for a job.

"I'll start you at twelve, and we'll see how it goes. Okay?"

She piloted the boat of an older Buick Le Sabre to South Laguna. Her home was just to the east of the Pacific Coast Highway, across from the head of a trail to the beach.

The exterior of the 1920s-era stucco house seemed in good repair.

"The living room," she said as pulled up to the house. "I want you to paint the living room." She looked at me through dilated pupils with eyes decorated in blues. Her cheeks sported excessive blotches of red, and her hair was a relaxed wreck. "You've lost someone near to you."

Somehow I knew she meant Dad.

"You are fortunate that he watches over you. He says that his hair is still combed back, and he doesn't need Vitalis to keep it in place. He laughed when he told me that."

"Who are you?"

"I'm Wanda Nichols. I can tell you haven't heard of me. I work with police detectives to solve murders. Well, mostly murders. I'm a psychic."

I wondered if I shouldn't have waited for Leonard.

"Come on in. Don't mind the mess."

I wouldn't call it a mess. One could fill an antique store with the vintage furniture in the living room. She seemed to have a penchant for items made of brass. There were plenty of doilies. Necklaces hung on the outside of some furnishings. A cabinet with a glass top and front displayed rows of rings. I couldn't tell bling from the real thing, but this looked like hoarding.

"I'm a psychic, but that doesn't mean I'm not crazy." She laughed. It was a friendly laugh. "You see why I need help. First, let's have some tea. I have this blend of peppermint and chamomile?"

Okay, this is getting weirder. That's my favorite blend. "How did you know?"

"The tea? Oh, that was a suggestion from one of my helpers. I hope you'll find it to your liking. Please sit over there."

I wedged into a chair next to a bookshelf. I scanned the shelves: Madame Blavatsky, Uri Geller, Krishnamurti, Edgar Cayce, G. I. Gurdjieff...

She said, "Mostly, I enjoy my gifts. I bring peace for those who are stuck in one dimension, and I pass loving messages between worlds."

I wanted to know more about Dad. It must have been easy to read my face.

"Your father. Right?"

I nodded.

"He's fine. He was talkative, and his stories often brought him joy. He genuinely appreciated the unique qualities of each person and every dog."

A tear escaped my eye. I smeared it on my cheek.

"It would be good for you to see him as a step evolved, a

consciousness higher than you last remember him."

"Where do I see him?"

Her attention seemed to have drifted.

"Mrs. Nichols?"

"What? Oh, please call me Wanda, it would make me happy. Peter, you'll know when you see him. Just remember to notice that he has evolved."

I hadn't told her my name.

She continued, "These spirit helpers. I don't always know what they're up to. In the last few years, they've wanted to help the police. The first time, they got me in trouble. All I did was tell the police where the body was, and how it got there. They thought I was a criminal. They arrested me! Now, they call me anytime they're stumped by a killer."

"Do you read the mind of a murderer?"

"Heavens, no. That would be confusing, even dangerous. I see images, that's all. Pictures that help the police figure out locations. Sometimes I connect with the deceased. How's your tea?"

"Good. Thank you. Yes, my name is Peter."

"Right. The woman who was volunteering at the day labor place told me your name."

That was a relief. "Uh, do you want to paint the ceiling as well as the walls?" There was a lot of stuff in the room.

"Yes, I want it all fresh."

I had heard that hoarders get uncomfortable if their stuff is disturbed.

She said, "You can move the furniture however you need. Some of it will fit in the kitchen or the guest room. I recently bought an estate, and it wouldn't all fit in my storage. I had to bring it here while I wait for another space to open up."

"Why not wait until then to paint?" Not that I didn't appreciate the work.

"It was time to meet you, Peter."

I felt the truth in her statement.

"I'm going to Los Angeles to help with yet another murder. There's food in the refrigerator. Eat anything you like. Why don't you spend today arranging the furniture and placing the drop cloths? Take your time. There's no rush. Here's sixty dollars on deposit."

"You're going to leave me here?"

"Yes,. I won't be back until after dark. I'm leaving this key for you. Put it on the ledge above the door when you leave. And please leave while you still have plenty of daylight to enjoy the beach. I'll see you tomorrow at Day Labor."

Wanda kept me working on projects for two weeks. I saved some money. It was interesting to hear about her work with the police and to learn about her helpers. She was a kind woman; yet, there was something tortured about her, a despair that found its way around the fortune-teller-turned-investigator facade. What happened to her?

She watched me as I ruminated, then said, "I was in a car wreck when I was ten. My mother and my favorite aunt died. I was left with an uncle in Bakersfield, who was far from nice to me." She stopped talking.

"Did he make secrets?" I had no idea why I said that.

"Yes, he did. I went inside when he...did what he did. That's where I met my helpers."

"If they are helpers, then they should help you," I channeled some advice. "Ask each of them directly what their intentions are. If they only serve themselves, you can send them away. Banish them. That's what my sister would do."

"Jane."

"How did you know?"

"Jane is your sister. She's wise and kind.

CHAPTER EIGHT

ALONE

SHORTCUT

NEGOTIATION

WILDERNESS

SHORTCUT

My body sprawled in the southbound right lane of Highway 101. This was not what I had expected moments before when I scaled a cyclone fence and leaped over a curb, intending to run across the freeway. I thought there was a break in traffic. Something was not as it appeared.

It didn't matter at the moment. I was on a dark, wet, dangerous freeway. Suddenly, it was as if an invisible hand rolled my body to the narrow shoulder—just a few feet of pavement beyond a dirty white line. A semi roared by, providing a nightmare view of its undercarriage and those huge tires. That was close.

Where is the curb? I felt the concrete wall behind me with my hand. I turned my head, and my eyes followed my hand. The curb had morphed into a retaining wall about six feet high.

Another semi just missed killing me. This shoulder is too narrow. The wall was a better option. I made a miraculous jump and found myself hanging with my arms hooked over the top of the wall. When the next semi raced by I could feel a high-speed swirling wind. As soon as it passed, I flung my body over the top of the wall.

Then came the pain. Getting to this place of relative-safety took all the wiles of shock and angels. Now my damaged body was free to complain.

I had met up with friends at the Coach House. Drifting Norwood and the Love Gods From Outer Space and the Moon played. It was Jack Tempchin's band; the guy who wrote "Peaceful Easy Feeling" and "(Slow Dancing) Swayin' to the Music" and many other wonderful songs.

When the show was over, I had a dilemma. I'd imbibed too

many beers to drive. My friends had already left. I was too cheap to pay a cab for the fairly short ride home. I decided to walk.

Standing in front of the Coach House I viewed the lay of the land. I could either walk down Camino Capistrano to the low-lands of Capistrano Beach then all the way up to my house on Calle Ultima, or, I could cross the freeway and walk about one-quarter the distance.

The shortcut sounded good. There didn't seem to be much traffic at the moment. It seemed like a good time to go for it. Over the fence, over the curb...except, as I learned, what was a curb on the fence side was a six-foot retaining wall on the free-way side.

I met the pavement with my right leg extended straight. The force of the collision transferred to my pelvis, which cracked in two places. However, I didn't know that, yet.

I laid on my back with my body hidden from freeway traffic by the curb. I wasn't visible from Camino Capistrano ei-ther. It was after midnight. It was raining. Shit.

I couldn't roll. I couldn't raise my shoulders off the ground. So I waved my arms. It was the best I could do.

The cold, the pain, the hopeless situation sent my con-sciousness into oblivion.

When I came to, two sheriff's deputies were discussing me. I thanked them and called attention to my nice clothes. And shoes. Let's get out of here.

"You know what's a coincidence?" I said, "Just the other evening I was at the Sheriff's house talking real estate."

They didn't seem to believe me. It was true. It didn't mat-ter. I was saved.

"What's wrong with you?" asked the first deputy.

"I think I broke my leg."

"Where?"

"Down there." I pointed at the wall. "On the freeway."

"I mean where?" He sounded exasperated. "Which leg?"

"The right one. I think."

The deputy felt up and down my leg like he was frisking

me for weapons.

"It's not broken."

"Peter," I offered.

"What?"

"My name is Peter."

"Well, Peter, stand up!"

"I can't." I thought about bringing up his boss again.

He grabbed my armpits, dragged me to my feet, and let go.

I crumbled in agony.

Deputy number two said, "Go ahead and shoot him. I won't say anything. They shoot lame horses don't they?"

Tunnel vision, then blackness.

I heard more voices. I opened my eyes. The deputies were still there, but now there were two Highway Patrol guys on the other side of the cyclone fence. They were arguing about who had jurisdiction over me.

"Hey," I tried to shout. "Please call an ambulance."

Darkness returned.

My body was horizontal. There was something on my chest. The ground was moving up and down and side to side. Oh great, I thought, an earthquake. That's what I need — an earthquake—with extreme pain.

This time when I opened my eyes, there were police lights everywhere. I turned my head. I dangled over the freeway on a stretcher. I tried to lift my arm, but it was immobilized.

"Why are you doing this?"

Nobody answered.

Out cold.

NEGOTIATION

Anxiety commandeered certain Memories. It hid them in piles of stones.

Anxiety demanded compensation for keeping those Memories hidden. It preferred obsessions and addictions.

Anxiety, like a Mafia don, insisted that it be paid first. It demanded to come before all relationships—before health, before joy, before love.

For my children and the child I had been, I needed to end this extortion.

In desperation, I went to the piles of stones wherein my hidden Memories were stored.

I uncovered a Memory. I observed the sensory data. I experienced the emotions associated with the Memory.

Frightened and overwhelmed, I returned this Memory to Anxiety.

After too long I tried again.

It took all of my Courage; it took all of my Faith; it took all of my Impatience, but, again, I uncovered a Memory.

This time I brought Compassion. Compassion had a message to deliver to the human I had been when Anxiety first hid the Memory: Unconditional love will shelter and protect, as the stones of dissociation scatter.

Gently, I observed the Memory. I owned it. I released it.

Ecstatic relief replaced a tiny portion of the demands of Anxiety, as this single hidden Memory was freed. Instantly there was more space for health, joy, and loving relationships.

One by one, I approached the hidden Memories. I summoned Courage, Faith, and Impatience—and always brought

Compassion—to retrieve what is mine to free from those piles of stones.

WILDERNESS

I chose to climb the waterfall. Logically, it was not my best decision, but this trip wasn't about logic.

My loaded backpack weighed about forty-five pounds. I planned to stay in the wilderness for about ten days—and I wanted to eat while I was there.

About three miles in, on the low trail to Snowgrass Flats, I deliberately went off the path. I'd been in the vicinity several times, and I had a good sense of the terrain.

I had an idea about where I wanted to make camp. A couple of years before, I'd pumped water with my filter at the high point of a waterfall at about 5500 feet. I imagined that I might tuck-in somewhere nearby, outside the view of other humans.

The situation was: first, I'd hiked for a few hours with a heavy pack and several extra pounds of body weight, and second, waterfalls by their nature are slippery. In other words, climbing the waterfall was a dangerous choice for someone tired, overweight, off-trail, and alone. Nevertheless, up the falls I went.

I wasn't insane; I'd filled out the information card at the trailhead. I even indicated the general area where I might camp. I had a compass and a topographical map; I had stowed them in my backpack. If I stayed on the main trail I'd pass by the most-used campsites, and, right now I preferred to avoid human interaction.

The best part of being alone in the wilderness is the absence of people. It had been too long since my last solo wilderness recharge. I daydreamed about one of the most interesting of those alone-times.

That adventure was on the north side of Mt. Adams. I was in better shape. I easily covered the three-and-a-half mile slog to a nice camp in about three hours. There was a nice level place for my tent, hidden from view of anyone walking on the trail that went around the mountain. There was a fast-moving stream nearby where I could pump fresh water. I could see the Goat Rocks for a while, but rain clouds were moving in.

Rain commenced as soon as I had pitched my little Mountain Hardware tent. I had rain gear. A little sprinkle wouldn't deter me.

That first day, after arriving and making camp, I explored edges of the high meadows up around 7000 feet. I found my way to the place where Adams Creek poured out from beneath a glacier. It was there I first heard it—a sharp retort, somewhat like a .30-06 rifle, from a distance. It didn't feel like a gunshot

The rain didn't slow. I gathered a few pieces of firewood on the way back to camp. It would be good to have a small warming and drying fire. It sure was wet.

In a sense, this was part of my plan. I chose the northern trails because they're less used than the other approaches to the sprawling mountain. Now the rain also supported my intention to seek solitude. Rain was not popular with most hikers and campers.

Back at camp, the view of the Goat Rocks had faded entirely. My view was grey-on-grey—the clouds, the drifting fog, the rain.

I set up a single burner stove outside the entrance of my tent. I rigged a modest shelter to protect my kitchen, with sincere gratitude for the absence of wind.

I made a cup of tea. It tasted delicious in the wet, chilly afternoon. I decided to follow the drink with a noodle dish. No sooner had I dropped the noodles into the boiling water than I had a visitor—the scruffiest bobcat that ever strolled upon that mountain. And it was not shy about begging.

Knowing that I'd never get rid of the cat if I shared food with it, I didn't. It would also be rude to others that visit Adams in the future if I allowed this cat to associate humans with food. And, you never know, he might tell the cougar...

I yelled at the cat. He wiggled a ragged ear. I threw a stick at him. He watched it, then moved closer—to about twenty feet away. Then I remembered my old trick. I banged a stainless steel bowl from my mess kit with the side of my pocketknife. Metal-on-metal. It worked on the cat, just as it had for more than a couple of pesky bears over the years. The bobcat retreated.

I dined. Occasionally, I hit the bowl. When I slept, I set an internal alarm to awaken to whack the bowl now and then. In the morning, I stowed my food in containers away from the tent before setting out to explore Adams.

Crack! There it was again: the sound that was not a 30-06. What was it? I was in a wilderness area with no hunting allowed, although I was considering a personal exception for aging bobcats. The retorts wouldn't carry that loudly from the national forest, where there might be hunters. What's in season?

The third morning on Mt. Adams, I stayed in the tent and waited for the rain to stop. It didn't. It intensified. I had two cups of tea. I read Herman Hesse's *Knulp*. I wrote until I ran out of paper. Then I scrawled on cardboard from food packaging.

There were three of those gunshot things that morning.

Cabin fever was setting in. I decided to explore some higher terrain. I pulled on my rain-gear and headed up.

Within fifty feet, I had a surprise. Two young women wearing shorts and tank-tops, each with a fanny pack, were running my way on the Around the Mountain Trail.

When they reached me, one asked, "Is Adams Creek Crossing passable?" She was jogging in place! The other woman was stretching.

"Not on the trail, but it's pretty easy to cross about twenty-yards upstream."

"Thank you." And they were off.

Did that happen?

Bang! That gunshot sounded closer—up the mountain a little to the west. For some reason, it seemed like a good idea to investigate.

I hiked directly up the mountain. More shots. I got on a snowfield and hiked higher. The field delivered me to the lower end of a glacier. Two shots in a row sounded. They were louder and closer.

At this point, I noticed a subtle upwelling of fear. I turned back down, and, as I did, there was a flurry of about 30 shots. This was not automatic gunfire. What was it?

Another flurry of retorts followed, then a sharp cracking sound—the shots and cracking repeated. I was nervous. Was the volcano about to erupt?

The moment I thought of an eruption, the ground shook. Yes, that's an earthquake, I told myself. Many of the Cascade mountains have earthquakes.

Back at camp I didn't hear or feel anything unusual. The rain continued. I made dinner. The bobcat returned. I hit the bowl. I slept.

In the morning, it still rained. I had reached my limit. I packed my gear. A bunch of stuff was wet, therefore heavier. I didn't care. I was done.

There was one car at the trailhead—mine. As I tossed my pack in the trunk, a ranger pulled up and got out to talk with me.

"Did you see the avalanche?"

He could tell from my expression that I hadn't.

"The head of a glacier broke off and triggered the largest slide I've ever heard of."

"I did hear some noises," I told him where I had camped.

"You're lucky you didn't pick a spot further west."

☯

The waterfall wasn't large, but it was complex. I studied every possible step; conservatively judging each for their propensity for slipperiness.

Choices for safe steps grew more limited near the top.

Damn, this isn't good. If I run out of options to go up, I'll have to go down. That wasn't going to happen. Ascending, I could lean in. The weight of my pack helped sometimes. I could visualize ways to recover if an upward step gave way. Going down would be treacherous. The weight of my pack could propel me into the air. Not good. I'd already decided that I wouldn't descend this waterfall on my return from the wilderness.

In the wilderness, things happen that I can't explain. Nature and my body work together, even when I haven't properly trained and prepared. It's as if the pace of my inner consciousness adjusts to the breath of the spirit of the wilderness. Simply said: I have a darn fine guardian angel.

My eyes passed it by at first. Maybe it wasn't there. Maybe I didn't believe it could be there. But when I turned my head, I saw what I hadn't before. A group of dry rocks, arranged like a stairway, wending off to the right of the waterfall; a wonderful, accessible path to the high meadow where I intended to camp. I walked up those stairs to the edge of a meadow. The meadow was nice, but it wasn't the place I had visualized.

I'd been on the Snowgrass Flats trail in the Goat Rocks Wilderness many times, but I'd never seen Snowgrass Flats. I'd always been on my way to someplace else: Gilbert Peak, Cispus Pass, Ives or Old Snowy. Also, humans weren't allowed in the meadow of Snowgrass Flats, so what would be the point?

I wasn't certain, but this felt like Snowgrass Flats Meadow. It was about 100 yards across. The wildflowers were spectacular. In bloom were snowgrass (of course), heather, lupine, paintbrush, anemone, aster, and so many more. They carpeted the meadow, rich and dense. I understood the prohibition against human feet; stepping anywhere would crush part of this explosion of bloom. This was the apex of an abridged season.

A slow stream meandered through the meadow. It varied from about four feet wide to eight feet wide. As it reached my waterfall, it looked to be about three feet deep. Water slid over the etched basalt in a mesmerizing play of light.

Bedazzled, I was slow to notice the other waterfall. It was

all the way across the meadow, and it was easily twice the height of the one I'd just navigated. I slipped out of my backpack.

Topo map and compass in hand I could pretty much tell where I was. I was pleased that it wasn't much more than a half-mile plus 250 feet of elevation gain to my envisioned campsite.

Internally, I heard the voice of WC Fields in *The Bank Dick* saying something like: "Lake Shoshobogomo is right over the top of this hill. The bad news is you'll have to get out and push."

I surveyed my options. One solution would be to walk across the meadow and take what was probably an easy route to the established camps. I couldn't do it. I'd harm the delicate ecosystem, and I'd end up associating with humans. I could go down the waterfall that I'd just come up, but that seemed deadly. I wasn't up to climbing another waterfall double the height. Steep cliffs shot up over 200 feet.

I laughed. It sounded weird in the silence. How fortunate I was not to have a hiking companion. If there were negotiations regarding the approaches to our camp, we probably wouldn't have taken the waterfall, thereby missing this experience of this meadow. Even if we had, faced with the current situation, we would not choose to climb a cliff. But I didn't have a companion. I decided to climb the cliff.

A switch-back pattern worked okay for the first part of the climb, but soon I was reduced to crawling on all fours. With the heavy pack on my back, I felt like a failed evolution of a life-form—destined to be rejected as viable, nonetheless compelled to live out this incarnation.

It was a miserable climb. As I neared the top, I collapsed. My face landed in the dirt. My heart beat rapid complaints. I had sweated much more fluid than I had taken in during the day's adventure.

I extracted myself from my pack without sliding down the hill. I pushed the pack a few inches, then a foot at a time. An observer would have found my predicament both ridiculous and frightening. To me, it was the only reasonable choice. I couldn't tolerate that pack on my back for another minute.

Then came the push when the pack began rocking, high centered. I gave it a good shove and pulled myself up alongside it. We made it. We were atop the cliff.

There were trees, not many, but enough to help create a hiding place. The ground was bumpy yet flat in places. There was soil. And water could be no further than the top of the second waterfall. Home free.

I was pleased to discover I had a second-wind after my traumatic approach.

I explored the immediate area. The trees quickly thinned. The Pacific Crest Trail was about 300 yards distant. Side trails headed down to the regular Snowgrass camps or veered up to the snowy peaks and the rocky crags of Gilbert. I should be fine if I situated my camp out of the lines of sight along the Pacific Crest.

Now it was time to second-guess. Why this attitude of isolation? Am I a hermit at heart? A bodhisattva longs to relieve the pain, the sorrow, the grasping, the repulsion, the attachment, the suffering of all. How could that be accomplished if one never made contact with other sentient beings?

Oh, come on. Am I going to judge myself, shame myself for failing to be a proper bodhisattva? Preposterous.

This was my retreat. Mahasiddhas and bodhisattvas took retreats all the time. Mikao Usui was on a twenty-one-day solo retreat when he received his way of Reiki, and a kick-ass satori to boot.

Hey, I seek nothing. I'm recharging. Ten days of solitude in my treasured Goat Rocks is a great idea. I'll return and bounce off people aplenty. I'm grateful that I can do this.

The first night of solitude stirred some fear. I suspected sounds amongst the trees might be evidence of a big cat. Bear were not likely to hang out this high in the wilderness, but I had seen a cougar at this elevation on Mt. Adams, at Graveyard Camp. Raccoon and bobcat would be more brazen, but maybe not. They might not have interacted with people. Marmots? I'll visit them among the big rocks in the morning. So, it might be a cougar. It didn't feel like a cougar, but this was my first night. My senses of place would improve with time. It was probably a bobcat...

In the morning the sky was big and blue. Ives and Old Snowy bounced white light as the sun arrived. I took a cup of coffee and strolled through the little forest. I was super-pleased to find a little clearing out of sight of the Pacific Crest Trail but with a terrific view of Mt. Adams.

I leaned against a tree and almost dozed off. My body felt pain in numerous locations. This was a perfect day to hang around camp. These muscles needed to settle down before the next push.

Again, on the second night, there was a noise in the woods. There would always be a noise in the woods. I kept my head-lamp handy in case I needed to shine it in some creature's eyes. It had an extra-bright setting that would...well, I'm not sure what it would do, but I felt safer because it was available.

The second morning I found a perfect hidden spot to pump water, just below the top of the high waterfall. My temporary settlement was established.

It was time for a stroll. I walked roughly parallel to the Pacific Crest Trail, playing hide-and-seek with no-one-there. I came to an ice ridge. It was flat on the top, varying from a relax-ing ten-feet-wide to an unnerving two feet. On either side of the ridge, the iced dropped at unbearably steep angles. There was no reason to calculate the consequence of a misstep; the result would be death.

The ice ridge took me close to Gilbert, the highest and the least accessible of the seven remnants of the crater rim from an ancient eruption. Here, a huge mountain blew its top long be-fore Rainier, St. Helens, and Hood began their reach for the sky.

I had a nice view of Gilbert. The routes I'd considered vi-able looked impossible once I got closer a closer look. Loose rubble didn't look like fun; climbing through fields of tipsy boulders would be worse. There's a way to summit Gilbert; I just hadn't found it. I hoped I could stand on that summit before this Parkinson's thing progresses to an assembly of symptoms that forever deny me that accomplishment.

Rather than return over the ice bridge, I scaled a saddle and happily glissaded down a snowfield. Several rocks about fifty feet in diameter, or more, scattered in the snowfield below. I saw marmot trails in the snow between the rocks, and then I saw the marmots. They were healthy looking adults, probably forty-pounders. They were not shy about checking me out. I sensed no fear.

I came upon the largest of the scattered rocks, about seventy feet tall and fifty feet wide. A vertical crevasse allowed entry to a cave within the rock. I imagined a teenager from a nearby tribe adopting this as a base of operations during his vision quest. I also caught an inner-vision glimpse of a benevolent traveler from another planet finding solace in this once molten gathering of minerals.

By the seventh night, I had difficulty accessing even a pilot light of fear. This was my comfortable home. But in the morning it became less homey. The temperature fell and continued to plummet as the morning progressed.

I watched Adams from my clearing. The mountain gathered clouds. It looked like it might rain over there.

Suddenly a wind came up. The tree I leaned against lurched. High branches of the forest slapped against each other like green applause.

By the time I crossed the short distance to the tent, the sky had darkened. Was there an eclipse I had forgotten about?

It started to snow.

It was as good a time as any to leave. This was my retreat, not a contract. I swiftly broke camp and made for the trailhead, this time by way of the gradual slopes through the Snowgrass campsites. There was no one there; nor was anyone else at the trailhead.

CHAPTER NINE

GAS

CRYOGENICS

HOGS

THREE-LEGGED STOOL

DO-OVER

BIAS

CRYOGENICS

In the early years of the twenty-first century, humankind realized that it had made a colossal mistake. Apologies could not change the reality that we had overloaded the atmosphere and ocean with carbon. The schedule for planet-wide suffocation was moved up.

Global climate disruption was no longer an inevitable future; it was the new status quo. Glaciers shrunk and polar ice chunked. Sea levels rose swifter than expected. The ocean heated and acidified—killing coral reefs and melting phytoplankton.

Solutions were millennial, or yet to be invented.

Hopeful dreamers expected a goddess, god or genius to perpetuate a miracle. Some simply disbelieved the overwhelming truth.

In a nefarious corner, hirers of deniers sought to profit from despair.

☯

Dawn arrived, regardless of any attempts by Congress to protest its legitimacy. Morning light blended with the chilled air of Washington, DC, and progressively illuminated the Lincoln Memorial, as I walked along the reflecting pool of our National Mall.

The memorial throbbed social justice. The symbolic fasces at the base of the staircase demanded strength through unity. As I climbed those stairs to meet with President Abraham Lincoln, each step firmed my certainty that all humanity and nature are interdependent.

I presented myself to the marble president. I heard him debate at the crossroads of ecology and human dignity.

President Lincoln's hands rested on pillars with more carved fasces, prepared to propel his lanky frame to a standing position, should his significant height be required to make a lofty point.

☯

I was in DC to talk with legislators and their staff about sustainable fishery management. My organization, Pacific Marine Conservation Council, balanced human lives connected to the ocean with the long-term health of marine ecosystems. We worked with the fishing industry, environmentalists, scientists, and coastal community leaders to reach agreement about policies that would achieve such a balance.

Meanwhile, back at home, mischief was afoot.

The previous evening I read the online version of *The Daily Astorian*. The Port of Astoria had voted to lease the Skipanon Peninsula in the city of Warrenton to Calpine Corporation as a site for a liquified natural gas (LNG) import terminal.

Wow, that was quick, I thought. Just a few months ago, Eureka, California, denied Calpine a lease to locate an LNG terminal there. My friends in Eureka were leaders of the resistance that persuaded the city council to deny the lease.

I was relieved when Eureka rejected Calpine's proposal. Now the company had a new location—three miles across Youngs Bay from my Astoria home.

What the heck? I hadn't seen a notice that the port was going to consider a lease for an LNG terminal...

☯

Calpine was a California energy company known for designing high-efficiency natural gas power plants. They complained that the declining supply of natural gas (methane) in North America limited the profitability of their plants. Other countries had a surplus of the stuff, but methane gas was a challenge to transport except by pipeline. However, methane chilled to minus 260 degrees Fahrenheit takes on a liquid form. As a liquid, methane takes up 1/600 the volume of its gaseous form. Load liquified natural gas onto specially equipped ships and you can transport it to any market that will pay the price—that is, if the infrastructure is available.

Calpine said they wanted to import LNG from places like Qatar to convert back to gas as fuel for their power plants. This was interesting, except the price of the stuff—after extracting, cooling, shipping, and regasifying—was exorbitant.

The Eureka proposal wasn't the first attempt to site an LNG terminal on the West Coast. But every community where a terminal was contemplated raised insurmountable concerns, including threats to public safety and the industry's incompatibility with existing businesses.

If a leak from a natural gas pipeline finds its way into an enclosed area, it can explode. This happens far too often with low-pressure supply lines to homes and neighborhoods, and occasionally with high-pressure transmission pipes like those that would attach to an LNG terminal.

A significant breach of an LNG storage tank similar to those Calpine suggested could asphyxiate folks within three miles or incinerate them if the gas cloud ignited. That could be me.

Methane in the form of LNG not only takes up less space, but it is also safer. It's not flammable until it returns to gaseous form. As long as the pipes, tankers, storage tanks, or conversion equipment don't leak, no problem, unless there is an accident, superstorm, earthquake, tsunami—or if foreign or domestic terrorists attack.

Richard Clarke, who had advised four US presidents regarding terrorist threats, called LNG tankers significant targets that are indefensible from a committed saboteur. Risks could be mitigated by keeping other vessels a safe distance away from the tankers, by securing the nearby waterfronts, and by detailing escort by an armed flotilla. Most important for minimizing possible casualties was to keep the tankers away from urban areas. Our towns, Astoria and Warrenton, were not urban areas, but they were our homes.

Armed protection for the tankers might reduce the risk of fires and explosions, but the displacement of other vessels—such as cargo ships, commercial fishing boats, and recreational craft—was a problem. Dangerous heavy industry would chill the emergent upscale tourist trade.

These were unapologetic not-in-my-back-yard reactions. Supporters of the development argued that critics failed to understand the environmental benefits of LNG. They claimed burning natural gas was less polluting than burning coal. Why not use it to produce energy as we ramp-up to renewable energy technologies?

LNG is not the environmental equal of natural gas. Factoring in the energy-cost and the expected loss of product to bring LNG to market makes modern coal-burning technology a competitive alternative to LNG-sourced methane. Even small leaks are significant to climate disruption. Methane is an atmospheric greenhouse gas with over twenty times the potency of carbon dioxide.

Plus, importing LNG is expensive.

I had to be missing something. The economics of importing LNG to the West Coast made no sense to me.

Calpine and the Port of Astoria held public meetings to inform the community of their intentions. At one I said, "It seems like Calpine was stymied from proceeding in Eureka because the city held public meetings to consider providing them with a lease. When citizens displayed overwhelming opposition, Eureka declined. In this case, Calpine and the Port of Astoria first agreed to a lease then informed the public. This way, public opinion wouldn't interfere with progress."

This was, of course, sarcasm, but one of the port commissioners smiled and nodded as I spoke. When I finished, he said, "Yes, that's how it went!" Either he was proud to be part of these undemocratic backroom shenanigans, or he was enthralled with the accuracy of my speculation.

In 2004, there were only four LNG terminals in the US, and they were rarely used. The only one where tankers passed through an urban area was in Mystic, abutting Boston Harbor. There, military gunboats accompanied the tankers when they navigated the harbor, divers checked for explosives, and shops and restaurants near the waterfront were placed on temporary lock-down.

Citizens of Clatsop County swiftly educated themselves about LNG, mobilized for public meetings, and learned about the permits needed to build a terminal. There would be a fight. A well-educated, focused community could challenge or block permits. They could delay the process for so long that the applicants give up. Maybe...

☯

A few months later, another LNG company arrived in the Columbia River estuary, this time hailing from Texas. Northern Star Natural Gas proposed an LNG import terminal twenty-two miles up the Columbia from Astoria. They planned to use the location of a long-abandoned lumber mill, which still retained a marine-industrial zoning designation. They called it Bradwood Landing.

Although Bradwood Landing was similar in substance to Calpine's venture, there were differences. The terminal itself had far fewer human neighbors, but the tankers would pass along Astoria's waterfront. Citizens quickly mapped the blast zone from a compromised tanker: In the worst case, nearly all of Astoria would incinerate. Casualties could exceed those lost in the attack on the World Trade Center.

Damn, there were two of these things. I figured that only one terminal might be built on the lower Columbia. But who knew? It didn't seem to make sense to build even one.

We needed affordable lawyers. We needed help from conservation groups. We needed an elected champion in Warrenton, Clatsop County, the state of Oregon, or among Oregon's Congressional Delegation. All we had was slim pickings.

HOGS

For more than 12,000 years, humans shared the region where the Columbia River meets the Pacific Ocean with mammals both familiar and exotic: from Roosevelt elk to saber-toothed tiger. Native people roamed the beaches and nearshore waters of the Pacific Ocean. They encountered seaweed and clams, otters and whales, seabirds and crab.

The relationship between salmon and the native tribes and families that catch, eat, and trade them is one of the most beautiful entanglements of human and animal. This relationship is not only one of subsistence and economics but involves a deep spiritual connection. The tribes and families of the river celebrate with great appreciation the regular return of the salmon.

Clatsop County has more area than Rhode Island but fewer than 40,000 residents. This idyllic county nestles in the northwest corner of Oregon. It's flanked to the north by the Columbia River estuary and to the west by the Pacific Ocean. A temperate rainforest sprawls to the south and east.

The most populous town (at 10,000) in Clatsop County, Astoria, adorns a spectacular, evergreen peninsula that juts into the Columbia River a few miles from where the Columbia pours into the ocean.

The Lewis and Clark expedition spent the rain-soaked winter of 1805-06 near Astoria and documented the potential of the region. A few years later, John Jacob Astor sent representatives by land and sea to establish a fur trading hub. In 1811, Fort Astoria became the first community on the Pacific coast owned by an American. Astor's fur company acquired pelts for the world market—primarily beaver and sea otter, with a smattering of fox and squirrel.

The Astorians quickly capitulated to British control of the outpost as the War of 1812 was brought to their attention. Astor's agents saw no purchase in fighting. The town was called Fort George while the Brits asserted command. It got a little complicated when the United Kingdom and the United States entered into the Treaty of 1818, which included a joint occupancy agreement for the Pacific Northwest. But what's a name among friends?

In 1846, the Oregon Treaty settled the situation. Astoria was officially within a United States territory. In 1859, two years before Abraham Lincoln became the sixteenth president of the United States, Oregon gained statehood.

Meanwhile, the international fur trade had declined from the days when fortunes manifest overnight. Many former trappers of furry mammals grabbed a homestead and settled in the Willamette Valley south of Portland—embracing new lives as farmers.

At the mouth of the Columbia, settlers looked around for tradable resources. They saw both the forests and the trees, and the cut began. Local sawmills refined timber for construction in Oregon. Surplus logs and those that fetched a higher price elsewhere were tied into massive cigar-shaped rafts or, more recently, stacked on ships to deliver around the Pacific.

Most of Clatsop County's forests were clear-cut; the resultant open space replanted to encourage a monoculture of prized Douglas fir. Soon, less than one percent of the original old-growth forest remained. Elk, deer, bear, and cougar still roamed the county, but populations of some animals declined precipitously. The marbled murrelet, northern spotted owl, and several salmon runs flirted with extinction. (A run corresponds to the species, the time of year, and the spawning destination.)

Federal and state pressure to protect endangered species forced moderation of logging practices. Between regulations and smaller yields than those amazing first cuts, the supply of exploitable timber shrank. Many sawmills and other businesses that depended on the earlier abundance closed.

☯

If timber was the skeleton of the economy at the Columbia River's end, salmon was its lifeblood. The red, oily Pacific salmon earned worldwide renown. Late nineteenth century advances in canning helped send those fish across the seas.

The Columbia River supported some of the greatest salmon runs on earth. The species known as Chinook had several runs each year. In the early twentieth century, the June Hog run brought the largest fish, with many exceeding one hundred pounds.

The lives of the anadromous salmon of the Columbia River Basin are biologically amazing. The fish hatch from accumulations of eggs, called reds, in specific gravels of unique waters—some in the main-stem of the Columbia, some in major tributaries, some in small streams or lakes.

Each tiny fish imprints the scent of the water where they leave the red. At the time they know is right, young salmon smolts migrate to the estuary, some traveling over 500 miles. They pause in the estuary to transform their bodies from a spotted trout-like creature, into a sleek, silver, ocean-going animal.

For as many as eight years, the salmon of the Columbia explore the Pacific Ocean, from California to Alaska. When their biological timer insists, they return, first to the plume of brackish water off the mouth of the Columbia, then into the estuary. The Columbia River estuary is a rich feeding ground for the fish, even though underpinnings of the food web changed with diked wetlands, dredged ship channels, and dams.

Compelled by their heritage, driven by an inner urge, trusting in an inexorable beckoning, adult salmon leave the estuary to find the place where they first experienced their identity as a salmon. If they survive the journey, they spawn where their ancestors spawned. Mission completed, they die.

This inspiring life story ended prematurely for the June Hogs. Construction of the Grand Coulee dam on the Columbia began in 1938. This celebrated feat of engineering was established at river-mile 597—without a ladder for salmon migration. The Columbia River is 1243 miles long. Somewhere beyond Grand Coulee were the spawning grounds of the June Hogs. Unable to return to their home waters, the June Hogs returned from the ocean to beat their bodies lifeless in futile attempts to clear the impassable barrier.

The June Hogs were not the only salmon run extirpated by a dam, and dammed rivers are not the only stressors on the lives of salmon. In many places, the natural riverine habitat is a memory. Human waste, industrial chemicals, and contaminated runoff alter the formerly pristine environment. The biomass of salmon returning to the Columbia River declined over 90% from 1890 to 1990.

The lower forty miles of the Columbia River estuary are still extraordinarily crucial to the remaining salmon, in both their juvenile and adult forms.

By foresight, miracle, or happenstance, heavy industry never found a toehold in the lower estuary. Now it seemed to be a possibility.

THREE-LEGGED STOOL

It was just as well that I missed the party. I vacationed in Hawaii while local progressives celebrated the election of three new members to the Clatsop County Board of Commissioners. One of those members was me.

It was May 2010, in the midst of the Tea Party movement. Although the offices to which we were elected were non-partisan, it was interesting that the three incumbents, who lost, all expressed sympathy for the Tea Party ideals. The victors were all registered Democrats. With a total of five members on the Board, that election transferred power.

It had been a wild couple of years in Clatsop County politics. There was one big deal: The county's electorate polarized over proposals to build an LNG import facility on Warrenton's Skipanon Peninsula and an attached high-pressure gas pipeline which would run diagonally across the county.

(Backers of the proposed LNG terminal up the river at Bradwood abandoned their project at the time of the election. An investment of over $100 million had failed to result in permits for construction.)

Oregon LNG and Oregon Pipeline were the last Columbia River LNG ventures to stand. Leucadia National Corporation owned both. When the original developer, Calpine Corporation, went through bankruptcy, Leucadia picked up Calpine's lease for a site to construct an LNG terminal on the Skipanon Peninsula. The principals of Leucadia were two New York City billionaires: Joseph Steinberg, and Ian Cumming.

Local supporters of LNG dreamed of jobs and money. They envisioned hundreds of construction jobs to build the multibillion-dollar structure, millions of dollars in local property tax revenues, and unquantified opportunities to do business with or receive payments from the operators of the LNG terminal.

Many long-term residents of the county dreamed that an LNG terminal would make the area prosper again. They envisioned high-paying jobs that require limited education; jobs that would offer young adults a choice to stay close to their families, rather than move away to find employment.

Opponents of LNG development imagined a different future. They envisioned the health and safety of their communities compromised, established businesses displaced, air and water polluted, and the awesome livability of the estuary lost forever.

I saw the discussion from a slightly different point of view. My work from 2000 through 2008 involved ocean and fisheries policy. With others, I sought to protect the ocean and marine waters while honoring human lives that depend on sustainable activities within the natural ecosystems. I believed, and continue to believe--a sustainable economy cannot exist except as a subsidiary of the environment.

I had spent a great deal of time in Washington, DC, helping to create and advocate for national policies that reflect this attitude.

I empathized with my neighbors in Clatsop County who dreamed of opportunities for their children. The county had experienced prosperous times. The seemingly endless supply of timber for lumber and plywood and export was limited. Harvesting and processing salmon and other edible marine life had once supported a dozen canneries in Astoria alone; now there were a handful. The boom lasted for decades before a broad decline. The natural resource-based economy was not going to return to anywhere near its former scope.

If not LNG, the proponents demanded, then what? Minimum-wage tourism jobs? The LNG project came with plenty of money. Sure it was dangerous, but the industry as a whole has a reasonable safety record.

The opponents doubled down on the potential for mass casualties, the danger of forest fires, and the mishaps possible when burrowing under rivers and wetlands to install pipes. Surveillance and increased military presence would discourage artists and shopkeepers, history buffs, seekers of fish and recreation, and technology-based businesses that value livability. An LNG terminal would change the culture of the area, for the worse.

It was a face-off. Friends opposed friends. Family members debated each other.

Initially, environmental groups kept out of the argument. Many organizations that worked to confront global climate change tolerated natural gas as a bridge-fuel to get beyond coal. They considered the showdown at the mouth of the river a local matter. Was it?

☯

Robert Stang was a pioneer of green development and sustainable business ventures. Originally from New York City, Robert got his start brokering Manhattan real estate. He moved to Astoria during the early days of the LNG controversy. Robert was the first person to open my mind to the suggestion that the Oregon LNG terminal was not about importing LNG, but about exporting the stuff. Initially, I thought the idea was preposterous. I asked Oregon LNG's representative in an open public meeting if the company was considering changing the project to an export facility. His overly emphatic denial made me suspect that Robert might be right.

Sure enough, estimates of untapped reserves of natural gas within the lower-forty-eight began to climb. The financial viability of accessing these reserves using a technology called hydraulic fracturing, or fracking, began to shift the energy supply paradigm. Fracking brought with it a fresh and extreme set of environmental concerns.

The Warrenton project might well be about exporting cheap fracked natural gas at a profit, not about buying expensive LNG from the Middle East. But the developers persisted in their denials.

The truth about the climate change impacts of LNG would be exposed, once the fracking connection surfaced. The Oregon LNG proposal was more than a local issue; it was a battle with world-wide consequences. The cumulative impacts of fracking for the gas, building new high-pressure methane pipelines, and widely distributing LNG could dramatically accelerate climate disaster. The developers had plenty of inspiration to lie.

I had filed to run for a seat in Oregon's House of Representatives. I planned to challenge the incumbent Democrat, Brad Witt, in the May 2010 primary.

When I realized that the LNG projects were probably intended for the export of fracked gas, I strongly sensed that I had a personal role to play in the international energy market. If we allowed an LNG project to move forward, this would promulgate unfortunate consequences for Clatsop County. Furthermore, life on earth would suffer as we accelerate the juncture-of-no-return for deadly climate shifts.

☯

From childhood, I knew what it was like to feel alone. Now I experienced loneliness of another magnitude. I considered my intentions, my motivation. Did I seek glory? Was I involved in this LNG debate because of nostalgia for places of my youth? Was that reason enough? Was this indeed a matter of planet-wide significance?

In early March 2010, it was clear to me that I should take pivotal action regarding LNG transfer on the Columbia River. It was also clear that the Oregon House of Representatives was not where that action would play out.

I made an educated guess that the Bradwood Landing project was soon to fail. Oregon LNG, with the unlimited resources of Leucadia National Corporation, was the most viable project.

A few years previous, at the World Dioxin Summit in Berkeley, California, I took a class from Lois Gibbs—famous as a community activist who brought out the truth that her neighborhood, Love Canal, was built atop a toxic waste dump. I was star-struck; nonetheless, I took notes. Lois described the three-legged stool of activism: government agency strategies, political strategies, and legal strategies. I shared this triple-focus approach with LNG opponents in Clatsop County.

With the help of Columbia Riverkeeper, the legal and government agency strategies were doing fine. The political strategy had mobilized residents and businesses to a degree I'd never seen before (although the community had fought off an aluminum plant some years back). The shortcoming of this particular leg on the activist-stool was the lack of enlightened support from elected officials. The fossil fuel industry had lobbied their positions for decades. They came with campaign money. Congress and the state legislatures seemed impenetrable.

Politically, the Clatsop County Board of Commissioners was the venue of highest influence. Permits for the pipelines needed to go through this board.

In a citizen-originated recall, LNG opponents had removed two of the five county commissioners who appeared to support Oregon LNG's project. However, the remaining commissioners were able to appoint replacements with a similar mindset.

The 2008 election put an LNG-skeptical dairy farmer, Dirk Rhone, on the board. I counted votes for the project. With Commissioner Rhone in place, it looked like four-to-one. Oregon Pipeline was likely to win.

In 2010, progressive candidates Debra Birkby and Scott Lee filed to oppose two incumbents up for reelection. John Raichal, a well-liked former sheriff, held a third seat in play. John was probably the most challenging incumbent to take on. He was also in my district.

With one day to spare, I withdrew from the race for the

Oregon House seat and filed for the Clatsop County Board of Commissioners—District Three.

☯

With two months until the election, I needed to move fast. Under the leadership of my campaign chairs, Lianne Thompson and Matt Van Ess, my committee formed. We strategized messages and planned expenditures. I raised money. Volunteers made phone calls and knocked on doors. Postcards went out in three batches. We identified our voters, our opponent's voters, and the undecided. We focussed on the undecided.

As the election drew near, I bought a significant number of radio ads. Each ended with Sonya Radford saying in a sultry voice, "Peter Huhtala: Local experience you can trust."

Oregon votes by mail. Each day, after the ballots went out, we went to the county clerk's office and bought the list of people whose ballots had arrived that day. We compared this information with our data, narrowed our efforts to convert undecided voters, and encouraged supporters who had yet to vote to send in their ballot.

It felt close. This election would hinge, as many do, on getting our supporters to vote. We did. All three progressive campaigns won.

Shortly after that, I arrived in Hawaii.

Since I won the May election with a vote count that exceeded fifty percent, I didn't need to stand for election in November. I would take my seat in January 2011.

Now that I'd earned the seat, I needed to figure out what to do with it; to understand how the county commission functioned on the inside.

One of the first things I came to understand was the concept of ex parte communication. If the five of us were to act as judges, it was only fair to applicants and opponents that we each had the benefit of the same information. Parties to the proceedings should be equally apprised of any relevant information that came to us as individuals, and have a chance to rebut or support the information.

Although I probably would have enjoyed the festivities of a post-election celebration, it was better that I was in Hawaii—not that I needed an excuse.

DO-OVER

Oregon's land-use system is brilliant in its simplicity and efficient in its implementation.

The basics were established in 1973 by Senate Bill 100, which was ushered into law by the iconic Republican governor, Tom McCall.

The state establishes broad goals. Counties and cities adopt comprehensive plans consistent with these goals, and the state acknowledges the plans. Local ordinances, statutes, and regulations support the comprehensive plan.

Most of the time, city or county staff take a look at allowed uses in a zone and issue non-controversial permits. If a proposed use is conditional, officials notify neighbors and others likely to be affected and seek their input. Should there be disagreement, a hearing might be held at the planning commission, or before a hearings officer.

If a party involved in the administrative process feels that a decision is incorrect, they can ask the jurisdiction—a city council or a county commission—to hold a hearing to review the decision. If there are still unresolved or disputed issues, these can be taken up by the state Land Use Board of Appeals (LUBA), advanced to the Court of Appeals, and, potentially, heard by the Oregon Supreme Court.

Elected leaders, such as county commissioners, have an essential role in this process. They have the last say—unless a party appeals to LUBA.

When making land-use decisions, commissioners become judges. (In some Oregon counties, the elected leaders are called judges rather than commissioners.)

When commissioners review a land-use matter, they examine the evidence and the applicable criteria: state goals, the comprehensive plan, zoning ordinances, and county statutes. They are expected to act in a fair manner, without bias. They can't ignore the rules and approve or disapprove a proposal without reason. Well, they could, and some do, but their decision would likely be overturned at LUBA.

There is often room for interpretation of the intent of the language in the criteria. Matters that appear to be less than explicit are often the subject of an appeal.

During judicial proceedings, applicants and opponents deserve fair and equal treatment. Each commissioner who acts as a judge needs to have the same information. Parties to the proceeding must have a chance to hear and refute any relevant information or opinions received by a commissioner or uncovered through a commissioner's independent research.

In contrast, when commissioners consider a legislative matter, such as a change to the comprehensive plan, they can expect to be lobbied. There's nothing wrong with that, and they don't need to disclose what they hear or discover. They can even be biased for or against the change, and vote however they wish. They are only accountable to their constituents when up for election—or recall if the jurisdiction allows such action.

It's not that complicated. If I am, as a commissioner, involved with making a new law or changing an existing statute, I can listen to anyone, read anything. There is no need to share my sources. I can vote as I please. I can proclaim my bias to the world, or not.

As a judge, I need to be conscientious about my interactions. If someone offers facts or opinions about a matter in which I act as a judge, I need to disclose this to my fellow judges and the parties to the matter--in public. The same goes for stuff I read or encounter through media.

As for bias, it is only I who can say that I will base my decisions, in a judicial setting, on criteria and facts, not on my personal preference. Of course I have opinions, even strong positions, but I need to set them aside.

We can disagree about vague language or the original intent of aspects of a criterion. An argument or vote in such a situation might favor one party over another. The best practice would be to clearly state the evidence and reasoning that precipitates one's decision.

I didn't want an LNG terminal on the Columbia River, personally and on behalf of my neighbors and every living thing on Earth. But I couldn't just vote against the idea; I needed to participate in a fair process. Fine, where was that process now? I was elected, but it would be six months before I take office.

First, the LNG terminal would be built entirely within the city of Warrenton. The city has jurisdiction regarding permits. There would be hearings there, but the county will probably not be involved.

Oregon Pipeline's project was in the county's jurisdiction, although they might try to claim federal supremacy based upon the Energy Act of 2005, or some vagary of the Coastal Zone Management Act (CZMA).

The CZMA has a Consistency section. If a state with a coastal zone has a federally approved plan for land and water use within their coastal zone, then actions that require a federal permit are required to be consistent with the state plan. The state plan can include elements of local comprehensive plans and statutes if they were acknowledged by the state and included within the federally-approved plan.

Clatsop County, for example, has an approved plan for use and protection of the Columbia River estuary. Part of the estuary is within Oregon's coastal zone. A high-pressure natural gas pipeline requires a federal permit. Therefore, the Oregon Pipeline project must be consistent with Clatsop County's plan in order for the state to issue a Concurrence of Consistency.

Oregon Pipeline applied for land-use permits to Clatsop

County in 2009. I'd observed the process as a citizen. While I waited to take office, I examined files generated by Oregon Pipeline, Clatsop County, interested citizens, Columbia Riverkeeper, and others—the sum of which is the "record." This record looked to be at least 10,000 pages.

The Board of Commissioners, except for Commissioner Rohne, seemed determined to do all that they could to approve the project. There were aspects where I believed that the majority of the Board lacked credulity.

As November approached, I envisioned that I would soon be one of the decision-makers.

On November 8, 2010, the Clatsop County Board of Commissioners voted four-to-one to approve the Oregon Pipeline project, with conditions. Suddenly, I felt like the election was for naught, that this project might go forward after all. I chose not to linger long in despair.

Rather than continue to pour through the record, I read LUBA cases.

On November 24, Columbia Riverkeeper filed an intent to appeal Clatsop County's approval to LUBA. On the same day, Oregon Pipeline filed their appeal.

I devoured the LUBA rulings. There had to be a way to change the situation, to get a do-over. I believed that the county commissioners had made significant errors. But I also found plenty of cases where the local jurisdiction received deference if there were conflicts of interpretation. A successful appeal could be difficult for an outside party, such as Columbia Riverkeeper. It would be far better if the other commissioners-elect and I could comprehensively review the permit application.

One example of interpretation involved land zoned for use as a forest. This particular zone included a provision that no new transmission lines could pass through such property. What's a transmission line? Did they only mean the sizeable electrical transmission lines that brought electricity to the county? If those who wrote the ordinance did think about natural gas pipelines, did they foresee making a distinction between a six-inch low-pressure line that delivers gas to distribute to homes and small businesses, and a forty-inch high-pressure line that links an LNG terminal with a primary interstate transmission system? The board, with three lame ducks, decided that the restriction did not apply. LUBA might give them deference because, as I learned in reading cases, county commissioners were often presumed more likely to know what was intended by their county criteria than some outside organization.

I needed an attorney. Because of the ex parte thing and general decorum, I didn't think it was appropriate to reach out to the lawyers at Columbia Riverkeeper. Clatsop County's lawyers served the existing board, for now.

I kept reading. Half of December passed.

There it is! Maybe? Hopefully? It says: "Withdrawal of a Decision for Reconsideration."

That's what we need. How can we do it?

I read more. Oh no! My heart sank. This approach is available only before a jurisdiction transmits the record of the matter to LUBA. The record was required to go to LUBA by December 15. It was too late. I was angry at myself. Why didn't I figure this out sooner? Why didn't I get legal help?

I dragged myself up to the fourth floor of the County office building. County staff had set up a small office where commissioners-elect could review hard-copies of the LNG record. I felt so dejected. I'm surprised I even went up there.

On the desk, right on top of the basket with the latest communications regarding the LNG project, was a letter from LUBA. Clatsop County had filed a request to extend the deadline to transmit the 11,754-page record to January 14, 2011. The document in my hand was an order from LUBA dated December 14, granting the request. I was shaking.

I walked down the hall to the open office where the Clerk of the Board worked. I stood at the counter. I must have seemed slightly dazed.

"Hi," I said.

"Hello, Commissioner-elect Huhtala." A big smile.

"I just want to make sure that I have the right date for the first board meeting in January."

"Of course. The meeting is on January 12. You'll be sworn in at 8:45 in the morning, probably by Judge Nelson. There will be time for pictures, so be sure to ask someone to bring a camera. They could use their phone, I guess. That will be an important day,"

"Thank you. It will. I mean, I will. Thank you!"

"No problem."

I returned to the little office and looked at LUBA's approval of the extension of time. Yes, it said January 14. Fourteen minus twelve equals two. Two days. Two days after I take office, the record is supposed to be transferred to LUBA, unless the board votes to Withdraw a Decision for Reconsideration. If the board takes such action during the meeting on January 12, then our lawyer should file our withdrawal on the next day, January 13. There was no room to wiggle.

The case law, as far as I could tell, was clear that a local jurisdiction could withdraw their decision for reconsideration unilaterally—meaning no other party could contest this decision. But LUBA would be compelled to deny the county's request if LUBA had already received the record.

For the next three weeks, I mulled this over, and over. I was ridiculously obsessed. Christmas, my birthday, New Year's Eve all passed—although I didn't notice. I was in a shell, lonelier than ever. It was exciting and terrifying all at once. My words and actions could be an important part of history, or I could fall on my face and let everyone down. Either way, I expected that no one would ever know what I was going through.

I was wary of telling anyone what I planned. I experienced a foreboding that the commissioners-elect (myself included) were in danger. The LNG project was worth billions. That kind of money can inspire mayhem, if not murder.

The first days of January dragged. I fretted that, even if the board asks for the withdrawal, something might go wrong.

Although I could see other approaches used for similar situations with LUBA, this made sense to me. Clatsop County should be able to withdraw a decision, especially one that could change life in the county for the foreseeable future. Voters had elected new representation and should have the benefit of our fresh perspective.

I had no idea what the other commissioners thought that we should do. I was willing to listen if anyone brought an alternative to the January 12 meeting. But if we go with my suggestion, we'll need to move fast.

By 8:30 a.m. on January 12, 2011, the meeting chamber of the Clatsop County Board of Commissioners was packed. Department leaders and senior staff were there; dozens of interested citizens, as well. Judge Philip Nelson began the swearing-in process at 8:45. There were cameras.

For a long hour or so we discussed budget policies in a work session. This was interesting and important, but I had other matters on my mind.

Many of the citizens and staff left once we got deep into the budget discussion. At some point, we asked the remaining audience members to leave the chamber so we could communicate with the county's lawyer in private. Under Oregon law, we were able to go into executive session to discuss litigation, which included the LUBA appeals.

A crowd formed in the hallway outside the chambers. When we wrapped up the executive session, we invited everyone into the chambers. Commissioner Dirk Rohne, who we designated as Chair (I was Vice-Chair), called the meeting to order at 12:40 p.m.

I made my motion. This is the way the minutes read:

> *In the matter of Oregon LNG Pipeline Land Use Board of Appeals case, Huhtala made and Lee seconded a motion that the Board instruct Counsel to file a notice of withdrawal for reconsideration of decision in a timely manner and that county staff prepare a notice of public hearing in which we'll consider and decide the procedure for a later*

hearing on reconsideration. Motion passed 4:1 with Roberts opposed.

The five commissioners sat at the dais. County manager Duane Cole and county counsel Jeff Bennett were at a table to one side. Planner Jennifer Bunch faced the commissioners at the testimony table.

It took me about two minutes to make the motion to return the Oregon Pipeline application to Clatsop County for reconsideration.

☯

No one knew what I went through during the months preceding. My solitary research, my second guessing, my worry that bordered on paranoia—none of that mattered.

A bubble expanded from the center of my body, first to encompass the eight people central to what just happened, then the entire room. As the bubble grew, I sensed silent applause. Ease of constant expansion joined with a super-personal tenderness in my heart and gut. I knew then, unequivocally, that this LNG project would not be constructed.

BIAS

The withdrawal took Oregon Pipeline's legal team by surprise. They intended to prevent this board of commissioners from ever proceeding to reconsider the erstwhile approval.

The lawyers suggested, perhaps even believed, that the county delayed transmitting the record because there was some sort of conspiracy. In an appeal to LUBA, they stated:

> *"...the real reason the county requested the extension of the record transmittal deadline was to give the newly elected county commissioners, who oppose the pipeline, an opportunity to vote to withdraw the decision for reconsideration."*

Nice guess, but no cigar. LUBA rejected that notion on February 17, 2011, granted our withdrawal for reconsideration, and gave us a deadline to complete that process by April 13, 2011.

Next, on March 4, 2011, Oregon Pipeline filed a writ of mandamus in Clatsop County Circuit Court. They argued that the project must be approved because the time to review their application had passed. They based this on an Oregon requirement that encourages timely processing of applications. Once an application is deemed to be complete, the county needs to take final action on a land-use decision within 120 days, or on a zoning change within 150 days. If the county can't say there was a final decision, then the circuit court must take jurisdiction over decisions regarding the application.

Clatsop County explained that the reason why there was

no final decision was that Oregon Pipeline, as well as Columbia Riverkeeper, had appealed the November 8, 2010, action to LUBA. LUBA now had jurisdiction. The circuit court agreed.

There appeared to be a conflict between the statute that requires a final decision on an application within an allotted time, and the law that provides the opportunity to ask LUBA for the opportunity to withdraw a decision to take another look. Oregon Pipeline asked the Oregon Court of Appeals to rule on this conflict.

The Court of Appeals used the chambers of the Oregon Supreme Court. The room is over-the-top awe-inspiring. It was crowded on the day that the Court of Appeals held oral arguments. A large delegation of construction workers wore t-shirts supporting Oregon LNG. I wore a black suit.

The arguments were fascinating. The judges skillfully drew the attorneys into the heart of the matter. The attorneys provided fine details. I was impressed by both sides. The energy moved back and forth. Many of the construction workers nodded off. By the end of arguments, I could see this going either way. I wondered if I had selected the wrong approach with the withdrawal for reconsideration. I got the vibe that our lawyers might have chosen a more predictable path. Just briefly, I explored a feeling of regret.

After the oral arguments were complete, I went home and waited several weeks.

We won.

The last two paragraphs of the ruling read:

> *"Because the county took final action by issuing its decision on November 8, 2010, the circuit court lacked jurisdiction to adjudicate Pipeline's petition for a writ of mandamus in March 2011. When Pipeline filed that petition, the county's final decision had already been appealed to LUBA. Because the county's withdrawal of that decision for reconsideration did not divest LUBA of its exclusive jurisdiction over the appeal under ORS 197.825, the circuit court lacked jurisdiction to adjudicate Pipeline's*

> *petition for a writ of mandamus and properly granted the county's motion to dismiss.*
> *Affirmed."*

Now it was October 24, 2012. May we please proceed to reconsider?

Not yet.

☯

As the pipeline case worked its way through the legal system, the project itself changed radically. In July 2012, Leucadia revealed that they now wanted the terminal primarily for LNG export. The cost of the terminal and pipeline was now estimated at six-billion-dollars. The stakes cranked up. This project might have always been about exporting fracked natural gas. My economic questions now made more sense.

The members of the board of commissioners were, nonetheless, required to review the application based on the public record as of November 2010; the rules of this engagement required us to disregard the change of the terminal to facilitate export.

On October 9, 2013, the board met to reconsider the application for the pipeline. Streets and sidewalks overflowed with practitioners of festive democracy. Our chambers exceeded capacity. I was now the chair, so I led the board through the quasi-judicial review of findings. It took four hours. We denied the application.

Again, Oregon Pipeline appealed to LUBA. This time they accused me of bias. This was outrageous. My metacognition is excellent. Bias is a personal matter; no one can make such a claim against another person. But they did. LUBA agreed with Oregon Pipeline and voted to send the application back to Clatsop County.

The commissioners could deliberate and vote again, this time without my participation. The vote in question had been five-to-zero. The county didn't need my vote; it probably wouldn't change anything. I would carry the distinction of one of the few people in the history of Oregon land-use proved guilty of bias. I didn't like it. But that wasn't reason enough to expect the county to spend money on an appeal.

Clatsop County appealed. The Court of Appeals agreed that the bias claim had no merit, and sent the case back to LUBA. I was vindicated, and we were on the home stretch. Maybe?

On April 29, 2015, LUBA finally upheld our decision, agreeing that we correctly denied the application.

LUBA concluded:

> *"We deny, in whole or in part, the fifth, eighth, ninth, tenth, and eleventh assignments of error. Our denial of the fifth, eighth, tenth, and eleventh assignments of error has the legal effect of sustaining a number of findings that the proposed pipeline does not comply with applicable approval standards. Accordingly, the county's decision to deny the requested permit approval is affirmed."*

A year later, on April 16, 2016, Leucadia National Corporation quietly announced that they would no longer pursue the six-billion-dollar project. They gave up their lease.

It was over. I let out a little whoop.

CHAPTER TEN

REIKI

OFF A CLIFF

ELEPHANT

MARMOT

CONDOR

OFF A CLIFF

"Chronic disease."

"Degenerative."

"Incurable."

The words of the neurologist echoed as I swiftly summoned emotional numbness to shield me from the surprise delivery of my diagnosis: Parkinson's Disease.

"Where did it come from?" I asked. "What caused it?"

"We really don't know. Sometimes it may be genetic. But you should understand," she explained in a practiced, clinical manner, "this is not a death sentence. You could live for many years with this condition. There are medications that help..."

I stopped her there. "I thought that you said it was incurable."

"It is. I mean it isn't. There is no cure, but there are medicines that help with the symptoms."

And what might those symptoms be?

I had asked my doctor for a referral to the neurologist because my right thumb shook, my walk was stiff and awkward, and lately, I had lost my strength—radically. I was forty-nine.

No, I didn't want medication right now. Thank you. I need to understand this. To be with this.

Incurable.

The neurologist filled my arms with pamphlets and magazines as I left her office.

I dug up all that I could about Parkinson's Disease: theories about the cause, what happens in the brain, the variety of possible symptoms, drugs used to treat it, the side effects of those drugs, deep brain stimulation (!), stem cells, on and on.

I learned how my MRI results and observation of my gait, reflexes, range of motion, and other clues strongly suggested Parkinsonism. I didn't want to accept the diagnosis, but I understood it. I also understood that the drugs used for treatment had problems. Eventually, they stop working. After even a few years, efficacious doses may come with debilitating side effects.

I experimented with natural supplements and herbs, ever optimistic that I'd find the right mix to slow this down, to eliminate the symptoms, to function more effectively.

Try as I might with natural means, within three years I was back in the neurologist's office. I couldn't type. I was lethargic. The tremors were persistent and impairing. I couldn't play guitar. Give. Me. The. Drugs.

The first medicine she prescribed had a dangerous side effect: I would fall asleep without warning, say while driving on the freeway.

I also began freezing in place, apparently a degeneration of the condition. I tried a different medication. The new prescription helped bury certain symptoms while creating new problems.

Soon I had four prescriptions. I ate twenty-four pills per day, and my overall health was in decline.

I lived in Astoria, where I served on the Clatsop County Board of Commissioners. I was engaged in the environmental fight of my life. I tried to mask the progressive disease, but that was ridiculous. Those who knew me could see my death approach.

Then I fell off a cliff.

Yes, I fell off a cliff, hiking off-trail with a friend's Labrador retriever, Finn. I tripped over a root and found myself airborne. I was within a bubble where time expanded. I had plenty of time to spin into a position of my choice prior to landing about twenty feet below. Once I chose a position, I was impatient to hit the ground. I wanted to see how it worked out. The landing wasn't bad. Much of my back hit, spreading the intensity of the blow and protecting my head. Then, I bounced! On the second landing, I hit my head. When I came to, Finn the dog sat beside me.

I wrote about this experience on social media. Besides frightening and entertaining my readers, I also received a comment from a friend from way-back, Deborah O'Brien. Though we were acquainted for some four decades, I hadn't seen Deborah for years. She understood the state of consciousness that I had entered during the fall. She recognized that something like a guardian angel had saved me. Her clear awareness touched me profoundly.

Three months passed. I was helping John F. Crowley celebrate his sixty-fourth birthday at Shively Park, in Astoria. I saw Deborah approach. She walked straight across the play area, then stepped into my arms. The embrace was comfortable, so natural.

Later that day, the electrifying kiss almost tumbled me to the ground. A few weeks hence, Deborah invited me to visit at her home in Portland. We began to explore the possibility of a relationship. But first, there were other matters...

Deborah was an energy healer with over twenty-five years of experience with Reiki. My neurological condition was apparent. She wanted to help. She had a massage table set up in her small apartment. I laid on the table, and she gave me a full treatment using a light touch. She drew pictures in the air. She chanted and toned. I experienced a deep sense of nurturing. My discursive intellect interrupted to allow a feeling of regret for a lifetime of missing out on such nurturing.

At home that night, I slept until morning. That hadn't happened for years.

Once a week for several months, Deborah treated me on the Reiki table. She later explained that she relied on intuition to choose techniques. She had faith that Reiki, an energy she spoke of as a wise friend, knew what was needed. The impact on my life was swift and substantial.

Deborah's intuitive focus on a section of my brain triggered one of my most remarkable healing experiences. She had explained why she seemed to draw pictures with her hands. She employed symbols—symbolic keys that unlocked specific frequencies of spiritual energy. She transmitted Reiki symbols through her hands and eyes, and by toning or chanting their names. This time she focused symbols through her fingertips. Billions of brain cells in a three-dimensional field extended beyond my body, beyond space itself. Neurotransmitters rearranged themselves. New patterns of energy flowed through them. Restrictions were released; positive functions optimized. I witnessed the inner details of effective energy healing.

The brain-healing process continued for several days. I felt and functioned better than I had for a decade. I nearly eliminated my intake of pharmaceutical drugs. It was clear to me: all is energy and energy is love. I knew by direct experience the path beyond suffering and spirit of healing. I wanted to live. Woo hoo!

ELEPHANT

In the summer of 2017, the West was on fire. Smoke from dozens of forest fires choked California, Oregon, Washington, and British Columbia. Temperatures exceeded one hundred degrees in some places; Portland among them.

Deborah, my bride of one year, and I plotted our escape from Portland. The smoke was too intense. It burned our eyes and hurt our lungs. To the north, south, and east it was worse. The smoke besieged even the Oregon Coast. We studied interactive air-quality maps and finally determined that a small stretch of the coast between Lincoln City and Florence, Oregon, was our best option. We were going camping.

We loaded our gear and drove through the smoke to the coast. The campgrounds were full. Maybe we weren't the only inspectors of interactive maps. Finally, several miles north of Florence we found a campground without a full sign—Alder Dunes. The park attendant directed us to an available site.

"Yeah, those folks left early, with the smoke and all," he said.

"Has the smoke been bad here?" I asked.

"It drifted over a bit yesterday, but it's okay today."

We pitched our tent.

Alder Dunes campground had a lake. We decided to explore the lake and see if we could find a trail to the beach. We found a lightly traveled brushy path, which eventually emerged from the woods at the top of a rustic sand-dune.

I surveyed the area. A hundred yards down and across the dune, the forest took up again. It looked like there might be some water there.

"Down there at the edge of the woods," I said, "there might be some Venus flytrap habitat."

"Okay..." Deborah was not as enthusiastic as I was about carnivorous plants.

"Let's explore," I said. We clambered down the hill.

☯

Deborah taught me the basic techniques and the master level of Reiki style called Holy Fire. I was particularly intrigued by a training that focused on symbols. I believed that the use of Reiki symbols had been instrumental to my continued recovery from Parkinson's Disease.

Deborah still gave me treatments, but I was also able to treat her. We worked together to train others in all levels of Holy Fire Reiki.

I completed my term as a county commissioner, as the last of the LNG speculators left the Columbia River estuary. My life had taken a sharp and unexpected twist. Instead of degenerating into a lonely death, I was healthy and in love.

☯

There is an immense amount of sand in the Florence area. Unlike the steep headlands to the north and south, relatively flat marine sandstone underpins this stretch of the Oregon coast. Sand blows inland for more than two miles onto the receptive landforms, as it has for millennia. In some places, there are long high dunes that invite all-terrain vehicles for extreme riding.

Our dune was on the small side; protected by a surrounding forest.

We reached the edge of the thick lower forest. There was no standing water, hence no flytrap habitat.

We gazed up at the dune. From a distance, the sand seemed undisturbed, at least by humans. When we took a closer look, we observed considerable disturbance: animal tracks.

Row after row of tracks identified the critters that had walked on the dune.

"These look like raccoon tracks," said Deborah.

"And here's big bird tracks."

"Some kind of mouse?"

"Um," I said. "What do you think?"

"Cougar?" suggested Deborah.

"I think so." They were clearly cougar.

"Are those coyote?" asked Deborah.

Definitely. I replied, "A dog of some type."

We walked among the numerous tracks, many of which we couldn't identify. Some snaked along small channels; others created a subtle background. Then we found the elephant! It was an Asian elephant, about eight inches high, etched in the sand. I looked around for human tracks. There were none except for the ones we'd left as we traversed the dune.

"That's an elephant," said Deborah, astounded.

"Yes, it is an elephant."

Near the elephant, a blade of grass with a bent top nodded back and forth in the gentle breeze, as it pointed out another form in the sand. We both knew what it was the instant we saw the figure. I knew its name and sound, and I could sense some ways it might be used in our practice.

"That's a new Reiki symbol," I said.

"It sure is," said Deborah. "That's why we were guided to come here."

MARMOT

In 2018, Deborah and I made an early season excursion to the Washington Cascades. In June, there would still be snow at the higher camps, and even on the trails, but at least there were no major forest fires. After a long drive through the Gifford Pinchot National Forest, we arrived at Walupt Lake. Only one other group of campers was present.

We spent a pleasant night at a comfortable site near the lake. In the morning, we were drawn to the Nanny Ridge trail. I had known about the Nanny Ridge trail for many years. I'd seen the path on topo maps, and always vowed to avoid it. The trail gained 2700 feet of elevation in about three miles, then sloped more gently toward Cispus Pass. The climb looked like a wilderness elevator. I knew easier ways to get to Cispus Pass.

Nonetheless, the path called. We could always turn around. The first quarter mile was a pleasant stroll. Then we began to ascend. As expected, it was steep. We had overloaded a single daypack, which I wore most of the trip. I had walking poles.

Maybe I was trying to prove something, to demonstrate that I could still climb a challenging trail. But that's not the way I relate to the wilderness. I wanted to go up Nanny Ridge for its own sake. It was unique and beautiful. I checked in with Deborah regularly to make sure she was tolerating the steep climb. She did fine.

Okay, there were a few points when I hoped we had reached the end of the steep section, only to be disappointed. When we finally made it to the ridge, there were snow patches. Nanny Ridge trail was a beautiful approach to an exceptional place. We wandered toward the pass until the snow slowed us to the point where Deborah found a magical grove of trees just waiting to join us in a ceremony. Deborah drew the circle and invited the beings of all directions and the master-teachers of pure love--archangels and bodhisattvas alike. Enlightened beings, attendants, and symbols perfectly assimilated in this perfect location where ridge met pass. It was as if the ceremony was the reason for the strenuous hike.

I felt great. The climb up was more exhilarating than tiring. The elevation and beauty of the mountains can bring on a sort of giddiness, I knew from experience. Going down a steep trail is generally more dangerous than going up. Knees, at least mine, are more likely to give out on the descent. I was concerned about leaving enough time to get back to camp. There wasn't time for mishap or delay.

We worked our way down the hill, sharing the poles. We were on target to reach camp before nightfall. With two miles to go, I spied a neighbor about twenty yards above us—a dark-colored mammal. Deborah was examining a mushroom.

"We should keep going. Maybe a little faster," I strongly suggested. What was the animal? I looked at it again. It moved. My concern was that it might be a cougar. But its fur was darker, almost like a panther. Well, it's better to move along. We didn't need to know what it was. I didn't feel like standing our ground. Moving along seemed the better idea. It was just as well that Deborah didn't know of my concern. I wasn't sure how she'd react if she got a look at the creature. With Deborah leading the way I was between her and the animal. I could fight it if necessary. Let's get out of here! It was bigger than a bobcat, smaller than a bear, with different coloration than a cougar. Oh, it was a marmot. Marmots are cute; they're no problem at all. I felt silly.

When we got back to camp, the camp manager stopped to say hello. I told him we had been up Nanny Ridge.

"That's a steep trail," he said.

"Say," I asked. "Are there marmots around here?"

"Sure," he replied. "We had to trap two pairs in the campground and let 'em loose in the high country."

CONDOR

Deborah and I walked on the sandy expanse of the Clatsop County, Oregon, beach. Sunset was imminent. Piercing yellows, reds, oranges, greens, and purples built mansions in the sky. We stood near the ocean's edge, turning to experience the awe of each direction. A colossal form traversed the sky and descended near the shoreward dunes. With grace and ease, a California condor landed on a driftwood log. Moments later, the condor leaped and rose. It spread its tremendous wingspan and moved on. The sun set into the Pacific Ocean with a green flash.

* * *

Made in the USA
Middletown, DE
17 April 2021

37671081R00149